CRYSTALS *for* BEGINNERS

Crystals
for Beginners

The Guide to Get Started with
the Healing Power of Crystals

Karen Frazier

ALTHEA
PRESS

For general information on our other products and services or to obtain technical support, please contact our Customer Care Department within the United States at (866) 744-2665, or outside the United States at (510) 253-0500.

Althea Press publishes its books in a variety of electronic and print formats. Some content that appears in print may not be available in electronic books, and vice versa.

Photography © Lucia Loiso, cover & pp. ii, viii, 1-4, 7, 14, 16, 30, 40, 50-52, 55, 57, 59, 61, 63, 65, 67, 69, 71, 73, 74, 116-118 & 170. For additional photography credits please see page 194.

Illustrations © Megan Dailey, pp. 25, 43, 121, 125, 135, 137, 143, 145, 149, 159 & 161.

TRADEMARKS: Althea Press and the Althea Press logo are trademarks or registered trademarks of Callisto Media Inc. and/or its affiliates, in the United States and other countries, and may not be used without written permission. All other trademarks are the property of their respective owners. Althea Press is not associated with any product or vendor mentioned in this book.

ISBN: Print 978-1-62315-991-7 | eBook 978-1-62315-992-4
R1
Printed in Canada

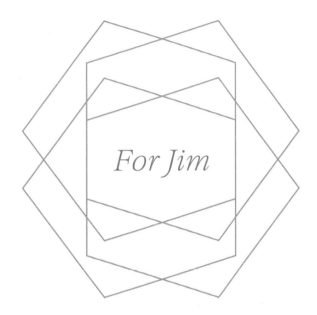

For Jim

CONTENTS

Introduction   ix

PART 1 An Introduction to Crystals and Crystal Healing

CHAPTER 1   The Power of Crystals   4

CHAPTER 2   Starting a Crystals Collection   16

CHAPTER 3   Using Crystals for Healing   30

CHAPTER 4   Maximizing the Power of Crystals   40

PART 2 Deepen Your Knowledge of Crystals

CHAPTER 5   10 Crystals for Everyone   52

Amethyst 54

Black Tourmaline 56

Carnelian 58

Citrine 60

Clear Quartz 62

Fluorite 64

Hematite 66

Rose Quartz 68

Smoky Quartz 70

Turquoise 72

CHAPTER 6 **40 Crystals to Know**   74

Agate 76

Amazonite 77

Amber 78

Ametrine 79

Apache Tears 80

Apatite 81

Aquamarine 82

Aventurine 83

Calcite 84

Chalcedony 85

Danburite 86

Emerald 87

Epidote 88

Fuchsite 89

Garnet 90

Howlite 91

Jade 92

Jasper 93

Kyanite 94

Labradorite 95

Lapis Lazuli 96

Larimar 97

Lodestone 98

Malachite 99

Moldavite 100

Moonstone 101

Obsidian 102

Onyx 103

Opal 104

Peridot 105

Rhodochrosite 106

Ruby 107

Sapphire 108

Selenite 109

Sodalite 110

Tanzanite 111

Tigers Eye 112

Topaz 113

Tourmaline 114

Zircon 115

PART 3 Improve Your Life with Crystals

CHAPTER 7 **Crystal Prescriptions**   118

Abuse 120

Addiction 122

Anger 124

Anxiety 126

Balance 128

Boundaries 130

Compassion 132

Courage 134

Decisiveness 136

Envy 138

Forgiveness 140

Gratitude 142

Grief 144

Happiness 146

Inner Peace 148

Love 150

Motivation 152

Negativity 154

Patience 156

Prosperity 158

Regret 160

Rejection 162

Self-confidence 164

Stress 166

Trust 168

Identify Your Crystal: A Color Guide   171

Glossary 180   Resources   182

References 184   Index   186

INTRODUCTION

We live in a modern world that places tremendous stress on the body, mind, and spirit. Virtually everything we do in our daily lives—from the foods we eat to our politics, work life, and activities—can pull our lives out of balance. Yet to be our optimal selves, we need balance.

Several years ago, I worked a stressful job for a company that didn't seem to care about its employees. My commute took hours. I had an active son and a husband with an even busier career than mine. With the hectic busyness of our lives, I sacrificed things I knew I "should" be doing: eating a nutritious diet, engaging in regular exercise, and enjoying activities that allowed me to slow down and seek balance.

Because I was constantly stressed and busy, everything in my life suffered. My health was poor. I was in chronic pain. My relationship with my husband lacked the emotional intimacy we had once shared. I was unhappy. I felt professionally and personally stuck in a hyperactive and joyless existence.

One Saturday, I had some rare free time and absolutely no obligations. I decided to go for a drive and wound up at a huge crystals and bead shop about 30 minutes north of my home. I was drawn to the semiprecious gemstone section, where I bought several varieties of gemstone beads and findings to make jewelry, something I'd never tried before.

Later that day, as I sat at my desk stringing crystal beads onto wire, a deep calm descended. My mind, normally foggy and active, felt intent and focused. I connected to parts of myself I'd almost forgotten existed. I noticed the stirrings of joy. Working with the gemstone beads created a meditative and blissful state I hadn't experienced in a long time, and I was intrigued.

While I'd always had an interest in crystals—and a profound healing experience in my thirties—they had fallen into the background of my life. I hadn't used them for years. Working with the gemstone beads on that Saturday reminded me of previous positive experiences I'd had with crystals and set me on a new path.

Since then, I've been collecting and working with crystals. I have them all over my house and use them in my own personal healing practices and with people who come to me for energy healing. They are such an important part of my life that I share my understandings about them in my book *Crystals for Healing*. While that book is a comprehensive guide to crystals, in the past few years I've come to realize that people who are just starting to work with crystals need a practical introductory guide. That's why I've written this book. It's designed to provide you with basic information and practical applications so you can experience the powerful shifts these beautiful Earth elements can provide.

PART
1

An Introduction to Crystals and Crystal Healing

CHAPTER
1

THE POWER *of* CRYSTALS

For centuries, civilizations have valued crystals for their beauty as precious and semiprecious gemstones as well as for the unique vibrational energies within each crystal that can help facilitate healing for the body, mind, and spirit. Societies throughout history, including ancient Mesopotamia, Egypt, China, and Greece, used crystals for their healing properties. This practice continued through the ages, although it lessened during the Renaissance, when people believed the healing properties of crystals came from either good angels or bad angels.

The use of crystals for healing reemerged about 40 years ago and continues to gain popularity as an energetic healing modality. In a modern age of science, however, it may be difficult to understand how a rock can bring about any type of healing. The answer lies in the vibrational energies found within crystals and how they affect the energy fields all around them, including the human energy field.

What Are Crystals?

Crystals are natural elements that come from the Earth. A true crystal has an organized grouping of unit cells that forms a unique lattice pattern called a crystal system. There are six lattice patterns that appear within healing crystals (see the next page). There is also a category of stones known as "amorphous" crystals, even though they are not truly crystals, since they do not have an interior crystalline structure. Some of these include amber, obsidian, opal, and tektites. They each have their own unique properties.

CRYSTALS AND COLOR

It's absolutely true that the color of a crystal can affect how attractive it is to you. But color also plays a role in the energetic and healing impact of crystals. We'll discuss in more detail how color does this later in the book, but there are a few basic things to know about crystals and their colors. The color of a crystal comes from three things:

- How the crystal absorbs light
- The specific minerals/chemicals the crystal contains
- Any impurities within the crystal

The minerals and impurities impact which light wavelengths the crystal will absorb and the color that appears as a result. For example, if a crystal absorbs all of the light wavelengths, it appears black. If it doesn't absorb any light wavelengths, it appears clear. Different impurities and chemicals/minerals affect light differently.

Crystal Lattice Patterns

The six crystal lattice patterns include the following:

HEXAGONAL crystals have an interior structure that resembles a 3-D hexagon. Hexagonal crystals help with manifestation.

ISOMETRIC crystals have an interior cubic structure. These crystals can improve situations and amplify energies.

MONOCLINIC crystals have a 3-D parallelogram structure. They are protective crystals.

ORTHORHOMBIC crystals have a diamond-shaped crystalline pattern. They cleanse, clear, and remove blockages.

TETRAGONAL crystals have a rectangular interior structure. These crystals are attractors; they make things more attractive and they help you attract things to you.

TRICLINIC crystals have an interior structure with three inclined axes. These crystals ward off unwanted energies or help retain energies you'd like to keep.

CRYSTALS, GEMS, MINERALS, OR ROCKS?

It may seem as though people use the terms *crystal*, *gem*, *mineral*, and *rock* interchangeably, which is common when discussing crystals. In fact, some substances that aren't crystals, such as amber (which is petrified tree sap), are also referred to as crystals or stones. However, if you're wondering about the technical differences, here's a quick overview:

CRYSTAL: A mineral that has a crystalline interior structure. Agate, which is a hexagonal crystal, is also a mineral and a rock.

GEM: A cut and polished crystal, mineral, or rock. A cut diamond (which is a mineral, crystal, and rock) is also a gem or gemstone. Amber and pearls are organic substances that are considered gemstones, but they are not crystals, minerals, or rocks.

MINERAL: A naturally occurring substance with a specific chemical composition and a highly ordered structure that may or may not be crystalline. Opal is a mineral that does not have a crystalline structure; it's a gemstone and a rock but not a true crystal.

ROCK: A combination, or aggregate, of minerals. Marble, which is made up of multiple minerals, is a metamorphic rock—a rock that has been subjected to heat and pressure over time.

Are Crystals Found or Made?

As crystals and gemstones have grown in popularity, they have given rise to an industry of laboratory-created gemstones. These are typically used in jewelry and often are of exceptional size, color, and clarity. They are less expensive as jewels than naturally formed crystals.

Natural crystals are formed deep within the Earth over hundreds, thousands, or millions of years. Therefore, many believe they have an unaltered natural energetic power. Lab-made crystals are formed quickly without the benefit of the Earth's energy. This doesn't mean they don't have their own energy. They still have the crystalline structure that retains energy. Some feel this makes the energy less pure. However, handling any crystal will change its energy, so it's safe to say all crystal energy is altered the moment it is handled. My best advice is to hold various crystals and see which feels like it has the energy you need in the moment.

The Crystal Electric

Everything has energy. In fact, quantum physics shows that at its most basic, all matter is made up of vibrating strings of electricity. So is your body, and so are crystals.

Humans are far better gauges of energy than you might imagine. Even people with little understanding of energy or energy healing might notice they don't "vibe" with another person. When you experience this, you are sensing energy and recognizing that someone else's energetic vibration isn't compatible with your own energy.

ENTRAINMENT

Have you ever been around a really negative person and felt your mood dipping just from being near that person? Conversely, have you ever been around a highly positive person and felt your mood lift? This is entrainment, defined as the tendency of one vibrational system to affect the other so the two move into synchronicity.

Consider your circadian rhythm. Also known as your "body clock," your circadian rhythm entrains you to cycles of light and dark to communicate to your body when it needs to sleep. All mammals have what is essentially a master clock located in the hypothalamus of the brain that responds to energetic time-giver signals to help them know when to wake and sleep. My time-giver signals are excellent. I haven't used an alarm clock to wake up in years because apparently my body clock is highly aligned with the signals it receives.

ELECTRIC EFFECT OF CRYSTALS

I'm a "show me, don't tell me" kind of person who enjoys knowing how and why things work. I'm no different when it comes to crystals. One of the things that fascinated me as I learned about crystals is their electrical effects, which I'll share with you here.

PIEZOELECTRIC EFFECT

The *piezoelectric effect* occurs when nonconducting crystals (some crystals are conducting and others are not) generate an electrical charge when put under mechanical stress. Quartz is one crystal that demonstrates piezoelectricity, which makes it popular for use in devices like radios, watches, and other digital integrated circuits.

PYROELECTRIC EFFECT

Pyroelectric crystals such as tourmaline generate electrical current when heated or cooled, according to ScienceDaily.com. The *Journal of Physics* notes that many applications exist for pyroelectricity, for example power conversion and infrared detection, among others.

EXPERIENCING THE VIBRATION

As with all other matter, crystals have their own vibration. The human body also has its own vibration and is subject to entrainment when it comes in contact with other vibrations. So, when you work with crystals, they can change your own body, mind, and spirit energies through entrainment; the crystal's vibration may change a little, as well. Because crystals generally have higher vibrations than the human body, they tend to raise your vibration. Vibrating at a higher rate is helpful for humans because it allows us to advance spiritually and move in more positive directions mentally, physically, and emotionally.

Crystals in Technology

Quartz crystals have been used in technology since the late 1800s, when the piezoelectric effect was first demonstrated with the crystals. Used to create oscillators that vibrate with a highly precise frequency, quartz has many applications for technological devices that require precision. Devices that employ quartz include sonar, watches, ham radio, and many others.

MILITARY RADIOS: In World War II, the military used quartz oscillators to control the frequency of two-way radio transmissions, according to an article in *IEEE Transactions on Ultrasonics, Ferroelectrics, and Frequency Control*. The oscillators were highly precise but difficult to mass-produce.

CONSUMER ELECTRONICS: According to the Minerals Education Coalition's Mineral Resources Database, manufacturers use electronics-grade manufactured quartz in computer circuits, cellphones, and similar equipment. CNet even reports that quartz in its natural form and other piezoelectric crystals were used in their raw form to manufacture an experimental rudimentary computer that transmitted or received signals such as randomized sound or light.

WATCHES: Due to the precision of quartz oscillators, they are used in watches, which require precision in timekeeping. Only a tiny piece of quartz is used, according to The Watch Company, but it oscillates so precisely that it can be accurate to a few seconds per year.

How a Person Can Feel a Crystal's Energy

You've probably heard of mystics, psychic mediums, energy healers, and metaphysicians who devote hours to communication with spirit, meditation, and other pursuits and who are highly tuned into the energy that surrounds them. I'm not suggesting you become that person. Instead, I aim to offer practical advice for the average person to experience shifts in energy by working with crystals. How can you interact with a stone in a meaningful way?

BE OPEN TO THE EXPERIENCE. I understand having a skeptical mind. When I first experienced noticing change as a direct result of using a crystal, you could have knocked me over with a feather. Not only did I not really believe in any of that stuff, but also, if anyone had told me when I headed out the door that day to go see a medical doctor/energy healer that she'd use a crystal to help me get rid of a persistent sore throat, I might not have gone at all. And that would have been very sad indeed.

SET ASIDE ANY PRECONCEIVED NOTIONS. Instead, enter the experience with an attitude of curiosity and without telling yourself any stories about how this may or may not work.

SET ASIDE EXPECTATIONS OF OUTCOME. I find that having expectations limits what I experience. Therefore, I try not to have expectations as I move into an experience, because the universe may have far grander plans for me than I could ever imagine for myself. Instead of setting an expectation for any specific outcome, allow yourself to be in the moment as you work with a crystal, and observe where it takes you.

START WITH A CRYSTAL THAT ATTRACTS YOU STRONGLY. For the first crystal you work with, find one that excites you. If it's one of the crystals I recommend later, great. If it's not, that's okay, too. If you find a crystal that really calls to you, use that one for your healing work. Chances are, it is calling to you for a reason.

Everyone's experience with crystals is unique. While I can share my experiences, in the end all that matters are yours. So I encourage you to try it and allow yourself to be open to whatever sensations you notice. Hold a crystal. Be in the moment and observe what happens. Pay attention to what you think, sense, and feel. Allow. Let your experience convince you.

From Feeling to Changing

What will you experience when you hold a crystal? It depends on you and on the crystal. Observe and notice what you feel. Pay attention to emotions or thoughts that arise, physical sensations, and anything else. Don't attempt to change or block anything. Just allow it to be.

When you hold a crystal with an open mind and notice what arises without blocking it, you experience stirrings of change, the shifting of vibration. This may be subtle, or it may be earth-shattering. Simply notice and allow. These simple sensations will set the change into motion.

Myths About Crystals

I work with students and crystals frequently, and I commonly hear certain myths that I'd like to dispel here.

MYTH #1: IT'S ALL IN MY HEAD. Working with crystals is designed to take you out of your head and allow you to be in sensation. Crystals don't require you to rationalize or explain; they provide the opportunity for you to experience. If you're worried it's all in your head, stop thinking and experience the sensations the crystals provide. You can rationalize it later.

MYTH #2: IF CRYSTALS CAN HELP, THEY CAN HARM. Crystals vibrate with energy that can entrain to your energy. Intention and mind-set play big roles in this. If you expect crystals to harm you, that may wind up being your experience, but this is true of anything. Your beliefs always play a role in your outcomes and experience, regardless of whether you

A Crystal in Your Hand, a Rock in Somebody Else's

Not everybody reacts to the same crystal the same way. For example, my husband and I went to one of my favorite rock shops in Portland. As we talked with the store's manager, he pulled out a tray of phenacite, which is a very high-vibration crystal. I hadn't encountered phenacite before, and as he set the tray before me (I didn't even touch it), I felt all of my energy lift up and into my head. For lack of a better explanation, I felt high.

My husband, on the other hand, felt nothing. So whose experience was more valid? Neither, really. They were just different.

In my classes, I frequently pass around different crystals for people to hold, and my students report the sensations they experience. Some are similar, and some are different. Two people can work with the exact same crystal and experience completely different outcomes. How you experience a crystal depends on your own perspectives, vibrations, needs, and beliefs. These factors will likely be different for someone else, so they will have a different experience. Likewise, you may have a particular need that a crystal balances, and your friend may have a different need that the same crystal balances. Neither of you has used the crystal correctly or incorrectly; you've just addressed different needs with the same crystal.

use crystals or take a placebo or medication. In general, if you approach the crystals with the intention of shifting vibration for your highest and greatest good, it is highly unlikely you will be hurt in any way.

MYTH #3: I HAVE TO BE SPIRITUAL OR NEW AGE TO USE CRYSTALS. My husband is the least New Age person I know, but he wears crystals around his neck because he's experienced significant changes from working with them—something that shocked him. To use crystals, you don't need to be New Age, spiritual, or religious, nor do they go against any religion or spirituality. All you need is an open mind and the sincere desire for change that serves your highest and greatest good.

MYTH #4: I DON'T NEED TO CLEANSE MY CRYSTALS. Because crystals tend to absorb energy, it's important to cleanse them to clear away any unwanted energy. I'll explain more about cleansing in chapter 3.

MYTH #5: EXPENSIVE CRYSTALS ARE MORE POWERFUL. Quartz is one of the most common and inexpensive crystals, and it's also one of the most powerful. The amount of money you spend on a crystal really doesn't have anything to do with how effective it is. What matters is how a crystal affects your energy, and some of the least expensive crystals may be exactly what you need.

The Beginner's Mistake

If you're like me, you want to know absolutely everything about something before you try it for the first time. You could spend the next several months immersed in information about crystals, learning everything there is to know, but until you try working with them, all you have is intellectual information. You would have learned a bunch of stuff, but you wouldn't have experienced the power of crystals. That's what I refer to as the beginner's mistake.

By all means, educate yourself as curiosity arises, but don't do this at the expense of experiencing. Pick up any crystal. Find one that attracts you. Put it in your pocket. Wear it. Hold it. And then continue reading.

CHAPTER
2

STARTING
a CRYSTALS
COLLECTION

I have crystals everywhere: in bedrooms, bathrooms, office, and healing studio. I have crystal lamps, crystal bookends, crystal coasters, and large crystal specimens. I've amassed them one crystal at a time over years. However, collecting crystals doesn't mean you need to fill every nook and cranny of your life with them. Two crystals compose a collection if they have meaning for you. The goal is to select each one mindfully, guided by what you learn from this book and others as well as your intuition.

I believe that crystals choose us as much as we choose them. Some may come to you temporarily to serve a specific need. Others you may use and then give away so they can help someone else. You might collect others because they call to you in their beauty, and they become a permanent part of your life. All are valid reasons for choosing crystals.

Take Inventory

Do you currently own any crystals? If not, go ahead and skip to the next page. Otherwise, keep reading.

IF YOU KNOW THE NAMES OF THE CRYSTALS YOU OWN

How much do you know about their properties? Read about the 10 crystals in chapter 5 and the 40 crystals in chapter 6 to discover other properties and practical uses for your crystals. If yours aren't listed in this book, the resources section on page 182 can direct you to online sources of helpful information.

As you expand your collection, consider adding the 10 "workhorse" crystals if you don't already have them. These crystals are so versatile that I believe they are an essential part of every starter collection. See page 20 for more about these crystals.

IF YOU DON'T KNOW THE NAMES OF THE CRYSTALS YOU OWN

While you don't need to know the names of the crystals you have for them to have a healing effect, identifying them helps you target more specific uses. Beginning on page 171, there's a chart of crystals organized by color that can help you identify your stones. Start there. If you can't identify your crystals that way, see the resources section on page 182, which lists online sources that can aid identification.

Once you've identified your crystals, take a look to see which, if any, of the 10 crystal workhorses you don't have. Filling any gaps in your inventory with these would be a great way to start your collection.

Where to Shop

There are many sources where you can buy crystals—both in brick-and-mortar stores and online. When possible, I prefer to buy crystals in person so I can hold the crystals and feel their energy, but from time to time I do purchase them online, as well.

CRYSTAL/METAPHYSICAL SHOPS

Many towns and cities have retail crystals outlets. These may be listed as metaphysical bookshops, crystal stores, or New Age shops. With knowledgeable staff, most will let you handle the crystals before you purchase.

CRYSTAL, MINERAL, AND GEM SHOWS

Traveling mineral or gem shows are a great place to purchase crystals and can't be beat for selection or price. You may pay an entry fee, and they are only available locally a few days out of the year, so you need to plan ahead. Most dealers at the shows are knowledgeable and will allow you to handle the crystals before purchasing.

ONLINE

You'll also find online retailers, including those devoted solely to crystals, like my favorite, HealingCrystals.com (see the resources section on page 182), and large retailer, auction, or craft sites like eBay, Etsy, and Amazon. Check seller feedback before making a purchase to ensure that you're working with a reliable seller.

Crystal Workhorses

While all crystals have unique healing properties, some are more powerful and/or versatile than others. In chapter 5, we'll explore these 10 crystals in some detail. For now, think of these as your crystal starter kit—true workhorses everyone should have.

1 **CLEAR QUARTZ:** If you don't know which crystal to use, start with clear quartz; it works with every type of energy.

2 **SMOKY QUARTZ** is the crystal I use the most because it's a manifestation stone that converts negative energy to positive.

3 **CITRINE** promotes self-esteem and prosperity.

These three create a powerful collection that will help you as you work with many energetic issues. However, for more versatile crystals to fill out your collection, add the following.

4 **ROSE QUARTZ** supports all types of love, including unconditional and romantic love.

5 **AMETHYST** helps you tune into intuition and guidance from higher realms, as well as the power of your dreams.

6 **BLACK TOURMALINE** is a protective and grounding stone that keeps negativity at bay.

7 **RAINBOW FLUORITE** deepens intuition, promotes love, and facilitates clear communication.

8 **CARNELIAN** helps you set appropriate boundaries, have integrity, and be creative.

9 **HEMATITE** is protective, grounding, and centering and can also attract energies you'd like in your life.

10 **TURQUOISE** promotes luck, prosperity, and personal power.

Crystal Shapes

In crystal shops and online, you will find two basic categories of crystal shape/types: natural (raw or rough), and polished (tumbled, cut, or carved). Many people ask about the difference in energetic quality between natural stones and polished stones. In general, natural stones tend to have a more powerful energy, but that doesn't mean they are necessarily "better." In some cases, people need the subtler energies from polished stones.

ROUGH STONES

Rough, natural, or raw stones appear very similar to the way they looked when they were removed from the Earth. While they may have been broken at some point into smaller stones, in general they maintain their natural form without any human intervention. In this category, you might see the following:

BLADES are long, flat stones with jagged cleaved areas, such as with kyanite. They work well as worry stones, which are flat, smooth stones you can rub a thumb along to help soothe you in times of stress.

CLUSTERS are groups of crystals, such as a cluster of quartz or amethyst. These are good for placing in an area to direct energy.

GEODES are rocks that have open cavities lined with crystals. They make great decorative crystals.

POINTS have one flat end and one pointed end (single-terminated) or two pointed ends (double-terminated), such as in smoky quartz (single-terminated) or Herkimer diamonds (double-terminated). These direct energy toward the point.

ROUGH CRYSTALS may also just look like rocks without any discernible shape, such as with an agate. Depending on size, you can use them for virtually any type of crystal healing work.

WANDS are long, narrow pieces of natural stone that haven't been deliberately shaped, such as with selenite. They work well as worry stones.

POLISHED AND CUT STONES

These stones are smooth and glossy. Some retain their natural shape with a glossy finish, while others have been cut or carved into various shapes (see page 25).

One Stone, Many Names

In recent years, some sellers have been giving crystals brand names, trademarking them in some cases, and selling them. Much like brand-name medications and generics, for every branded crystal, there's typically a far less expensive "generic" version that has the same properties. There is no difference between brand-name crystals and their nonbranded counterparts other than price. Typically, the reason it is branded is because it comes from a particular area on property owned by the people branding it, but location doesn't affect the properties of the crystal much, if at all.

+ Amazon Jade is amazonite.

+ Aqua Terra Jasper is either resin or onyx.

+ Atlantis Stone is Larimar.

+ Azeztulite is and has the same properties as clear quartz.

+ Boji Stones can also be found nonbranded as Kansas pop rocks or concretion stones.

+ Healerite is generically found as chrysolite.

+ Isis Calcite is the branded form of white calcite.

+ Lemurian Light Crystals are a branded form of lemurian quartz.

+ Mani Stone is black-and-white jasper.

- Master Shamanite is the same as black calcite.

- Merkabite Calcite is white calcite.

- Revelation Stone is brown or red jasper.

- Sauralite Azeztulite is quartz from New Zealand.

- Zultanite is the mineral diaspore.

- Agape Crystals are a combination of seven different crystals: clear quartz, smoky quartz, rutilated quartz, amethyst, goethite, lepidocrosite, and cacoxenite.

Finding Your Crystal

Earlier I mentioned 10 crystal workhorses, as well as suggesting the top three of those. That doesn't mean you have to buy those crystals. If you're looking for a crystal for a specific issue, I recommend checking out chapter 7 for ideas. However, there are other ways you can find crystals that will work for you, as well.

CHOOSE BY CRYSTAL SYSTEM

Each crystal is part of a different crystal system with certain properties. In chapters 5 and 6, you'll find the crystal system listed for each. The crystal systems include

- Hexagonal crystals, which manifest

- Isometric crystals, which improve situations and amplify energies

- Monoclinic crystals, which protect and safeguard

- Orthorhombic crystals, which cleanse, clear, unblock, and release

- Tetragonal crystals, which attract

The Sacred Geometry of Cut Stones

You can find crystals cut into many different shapes, including spheres and polyhedrons, which have varying properties. Working with stones cut into these shapes will impart the properties of both the crystal and the sacred shape.

 DODECAHEDRON The dodecahedron is associated with the element of the Ethers and connects you to intuition and higher realms.

 HEXAHEDRON The hexahedron, or cube, represents the element of Earth. It is grounding and stable.

 ICOSAHEDRON The icosahedron is linked to the element of Water. It connects you to change and flow.

 MERKABA The merkaba is a 3-D star. It contains all five of the above polyhedrons within it and therefore combines all the effects of each. It is also associated with the energy of sacred truth and eternal wisdom.

 OCTAHEDRON The octahedron represents the element of Air and promotes compassion, kindness, forgiveness, and love.

 SPHERE The sphere has the energy of completeness, wholeness, and oneness.

 TETRAHEDRON Associated with the element of Fire, a tetrahedron (pyramid) promotes balance, stability, and the ability to create change.

- Triclinic crystals, which contain or ward off energies
- Amorphous "crystals," which have differing properties

CHOOSE BY COLOR

The importance of color extends far beyond personal preference. Each color has its own vibrational energies with associated healing properties. We'll discuss the various properties of color in the next chapter. However, by choosing a crystal of the crystal system that has the properties you'd like it to display along with the healing principles of the color, you can select crystals quite specifically for certain conditions.

CHOOSE BY HOW THEY MAKE YOU FEEL

I choose crystals by intuition. Whenever possible, I hold them in my hand and notice how they make me feel. I note whether they make me feel comfortable or uncomfortable, if they feel heavy or light in my hand, and any other sensations that arise. If I find it a pleasing sensation, I buy the crystal. If I don't, I leave it.

That's not to say that once a crystal has given you an unpleasant sensation, you should never revisit that type of crystal. As your needs change, so will the crystals that resonate with you. Pay attention to any attraction you feel toward crystals apart from how they look, and if one calls to you, trust it is a crystal that is choosing you.

Pairing Crystals

Like wine and food, some crystals pair well to make them better than the sum of their parts. Crystals that pair well have complementary energies that can really help focus energy. For example, the energy of any crystal is amplified when paired with clear quartz. Here are some other pairings that work well:

 **SMOKY QUARTZ + APACHE TEARS** (a type of obsidian) is a powerful combination for people who are grieving. Apache tears help you process grief while smoky quartz transmutes negative energy to positive.

 **AMETHYST + LABRADORITE** can help you have a more restful night's sleep. Amethyst is excellent for insomnia, while labradorite calms nightmares and promotes good dreams.

 **CITRINE + BLACK TOURMALINE** can help ground you in prosperity. Citrine is a stone of prosperity, while black tourmaline is grounding and also blocks negative energy, which can help remove thoughts that prevent prosperity.

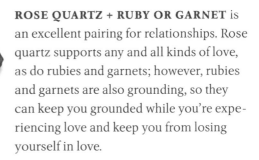 **ROSE QUARTZ + RUBY OR GARNET** is an excellent pairing for relationships. Rose quartz supports any and all kinds of love, as do rubies and garnets; however, rubies and garnets are also grounding, so they can keep you grounded while you're experiencing love and keep you from losing yourself in love.

 **BLACK TOURMALINE + CLEAR QUARTZ** balance masculine and feminine energies and can help facilitate the free flow of balanced energy.

Cave of Crystals

If you're looking for the largest crystals on the planet, you'll find them in the Cueva de los Cristales (Cave of Crystals) in Chihuahua, Mexico. The giant crystal-filled cave is home to enormous selenite (gypsum) crystals and was discovered in 2000 when two brothers were drilling in the Naica mine about 1,000 feet below the ground.

The Cave of Crystals houses huge luminescent crystals rising from floor to ceiling in the main cavern. This one-of-a-kind cave has crystals more than 30 feet long, with the largest being 39 feet long and 13 feet in diameter and weighing around 55 tons. The crystals have grown to be the largest in the world due to the combination of heat and humidity. The air temperature gets up to 138°F with 99 percent humidity.

Seven Tips for Crystal Shopping

For me, crystal shopping is a destination activity. I make a day of it, and I love poking through shops and finding crystals that appeal to me. Here are my top tips for buying crystals in person:

/ **Ground yourself before you go.** Many people find that the energy in crystal shops can feel disorienting. Before you enter the crystal shop, close your eyes and visualize roots growing from your feet into the Earth. If you feel lightheaded while in the shop, pick up a black stone and hold it until the feeling ceases.

2 **Ask questions.** If you go to a gem show, a gem fair, or a shop that specializes in crystals, chances are there are experts available to help you find the right crystal. Most of them love it when you ask questions, and it's a great way to educate yourself. Make use of this valuable resource.

3 **Go where you are drawn.** Pay attention, and if you feel drawn to a certain location within the shop, go there. Then see which crystal draws you. It's a great way to bring the intuitive process into your crystal shopping.

4 **Touch the crystals.** When in a crystal shop, always hold crystals before you buy them, to see how they make you feel. If the shop won't allow you to touch or hold crystals before buying, find a different place to shop.

5 **Check a seller's reputation.** Do a little research before you buy. For brick-and-mortar stores, check sites like Yelp or ask for recommendations. Online, check the seller's reputation by reading the reviews.

6 **Don't buy the first thing you see.** When surrounded by shiny objects, it's easy to get overwhelmed or overly excited and grab the first pretty, sparkly thing that catches your eye. I get it! Shop around. This is especially true at gem and mineral shows. Compare prices from vendor to vendor to find the best price for the crystal that most appeals to you.

7 **Don't be conned by trademarked crystals.** If you don't recognize a crystal name, ask the vendor if it's trademarked. If it is, seek the generic version. Look it up online or on your smartphone to get more information about it. You can also use a smartphone app to learn whether it's a trademarked crystal or a less expensive generic version (search "Healing Crystals" in an app store).

CHAPTER
3

USING CRYSTALS *for* HEALING

You are more than a body. You are also a mind/emotions and have a spiritual aspect some people call their higher self or soul. Energy flows between these three aspects of you. To be truly healthy in every way, it is essential to attend to all three aspects. Health in your body, mind, and spirit arises from the optimal balanced energy flow in all three areas. For energy to be balanced, you need to remove or absorb energy where it is in excess, increase energy where there is too little, remove blockages where energy can't flow, and vibrate at a frequency that is aligned with optimal health of body, mind, and spirit. Crystals can adjust energy flow in all of these ways to help optimize your well-being.

What Crystals Can Heal

So how exactly can a crystal heal, and what type of healing can it do? In truth, crystals don't cause healing. Rather, they vibrate with energy your body entrains with and/or absorbs, and it is you who do the healing by drawing in that energy.

BODY

Your body is the physical aspect of you. Crystals can help balance bodily energies and bring about physical changes. These might include things such as relieving headaches, low energy and exhaustion, and similar bodily ailments. I've even had crystals cure a persistent sore throat. (Caution: Never use crystals internally, and don't substitute the use of crystals for care from a qualified healthcare provider.)

MIND

Your mind is both physical (brain and nervous system) and nonphysical (emotions, dreams, thoughts, etc.). The vibration in crystals can help balance energies of the mind to bring about healing. Conditions that can be eased might include stress, emotional issues, insomnia, nightmares, anxiety, depression, grief, and lack of enthusiasm.

SPIRIT

Your spirit is the part of you that is purely nonphysical. Crystals can assist in balancing spiritual energies such as beliefs, unconditional love, forgiveness, and compassion. They can also facilitate communication with your higher self/soul or a higher power.

Cleansing Crystals

Just as you can entrain to the energy of a crystal, a crystal can entrain to the energies around it. So anytime someone handles a crystal or it changes location, or even if it is just sitting in the emotional environment of your home, the crystal's vibrational energies may change slightly. To counteract this effect, it's important to cleanse crystals regularly. Any method will work, although I prefer sound or sage for their convenience.

LEAVE THEM IN MOONLIGHT. Moonlight is cleansing for crystals. Set your crystals on a windowsill or outdoors overnight.

CLEANSE THEM IN A BED OF QUARTZ. If you have a large quartz geode, place smaller crystals inside the geode for 12 to 24 hours.

USE SOUND. I have crystal singing bowls and brass singing bowls. If you have them, bring the singing bowl to ringing and then hold the crystals within the sound field.

USE SMOKING SAGE. Light a sage bundle or smudge stick and allow the smoke to drift over the crystals. This is an excellent way to cleanse a bunch of crystals at once and one of my preferred methods of cleansing.

SALT OR WATER CLEANSING. You will often see people recommending cleansing crystals in sea salt, water, or saltwater. I don't, because salt, water, or saltwater will damage certain crystals. You should never cleanse any raw or natural crystal in salt, water, or saltwater. Other crystals you should never cleanse this way include:

- Amber
- Calcite
- Kyanite
- Malachite
- Moonstone
- Opal
- Selenite
- Topaz

Programming Crystals

When working with energy, intention plays a big role. While it is not necessary to do so, you can program freshly cleansed crystals with intent if you wish to work with a specific energy. This can be especially helpful if you only have a few crystals. For example, clear quartz works with virtually every energy, but when you program it with intent, it makes the crystal even more powerful. To program a crystal:

HOLD IT IN YOUR GIVING (DOMINANT) HAND. Close your eyes and picture your intent. For example, if your intent is prosperity, repeat the affirmation, "I am prosperous" as you hold your crystal.

IMAGINE YOUR INTENT TURNING TO LIGHT and traveling through your arm, into your hand, and into your crystal. Do this for three to five minutes.

Maintaining Crystals

Crystal maintenance keeps your crystals in good physical condition and also protects their highest possible vibratory state. To maintain your crystals:

CLEANSE THEM AT LEAST ONCE A MONTH. I recommend doing it every full moon, which can help you remember to do so. You should also cleanse after heavy use and when you first bring them home.

STORE THEM CAREFULLY. Storing them individually wrapped can keep them from getting scratched and maintain their vibrational energies.

IF YOU DISPLAY CRYSTALS, DUST THEM WITH A SOFT CLOTH. A soft microfiber or cotton cloth works well here, or you can use a feather-style duster. Avoid any cloth that is too abrasive.

Choosing a Crystal to Use

If your crystal collection has grown, how do you know which to use? There are several ways to choose.

ASK, "WHICH CRYSTAL DO I NEED?" AND LISTEN FOR THE ANSWER. This is my preferred method because sometimes what I think needs healing isn't actually what needs healing. Asking removes any preconceived notions.

DIG THROUGH THE CRYSTAL PROPERTIES AND CONDITIONS IN THIS BOOK OR ONLINE. Choose the crystal based on color and crystal system. Use your best knowledge to guide you to a crystal that's right in that moment.

USE MUSCLE TESTING. Place a crystal somewhere on you. Then, with your giving (dominant) hand, extend your pointer finger and press down on it with your middle finger of the *same* hand, resisting with your pointer finger. If you hold strong, you don't need that crystal right now. If you can't hold strong, that is the crystal to work with.

GO WITH YOUR GUT. Choose the crystal that calls to you.

Practical Tips for Using Crystals

You can use crystals in many ways. One common method is to hold them in your hand or place them on your body and meditate, but there are others, as well. Of course, there are tips in the specific crystals and conditions sections of this book so you'll know how to use them, but the tips here offer additional practical suggestions for applied use.

/ Make crystal elixirs. Set clean, cleansed crystals in a bowl of spring water in the sunlight for two hours. Remove the crystals and drink the water as needed. Don't use any of the crystals listed in the Crystal

Safety section on page 38, and make sure any crystals you use are free of debris, dust, and dirt.

2   Tape a piece of fluorite to the bottom of your work chair to help you stay focused.

3   On days when you need a boost of creativity, carry carnelian in a pants pocket or wear it as a bracelet.

4   Going on a first date, proposing, or engaging in another romantic activity you want to go well? Wear rose quartz as a long pendant so the quartz hangs right over your heart center.

5   Drop water-safe crystals in your bathwater. Remove them before draining the bathtub.

6   Feeling negative or need an energetic boost? Amber is the perfect crystal to boost both happiness and energy. Wear it close to the skin—as a bracelet or ring especially—to give yourself a boost.

7   Sprinkle positive energy crystals, such as smoky quartz, or crystals that absorb negative energy, such as black tourmaline, around the perimeter of your property or home to keep negativity at bay. You can use inexpensive crystal chips or beads for this purpose.

The Change You Can Expect

When we do energy work, the energy always seeks to align with our highest and greatest good. Sometimes the change you think you need isn't what best serves you. Remove any expectation of the outcome and allow what serves you to arise. When we set expectations and stick to them, we limit results, because what we imagine is usually smaller than what the universe provides. And sometimes what serves our greatest good doesn't appear as we think it should.

Setting an Intention

In all of the energy healing work I do, I often say, "Intention is everything." Your mind is a powerful driver of your reality. Thoughts, words, and actions affect what you are able to manifest, and this always starts with intention.

Setting an intention is a powerful aspect of working with crystal healing. The use of crystals to heal specific issues is actually unspoken intent to bring about healing in some aspect of yourself. Defining and giving voice to the intent renders it more powerful.

Creating intent is easy. Decide what it is you wish to experience or be, then make a statement of intent as if you have already achieved that. Using the example of prosperity again, affirm "I am prosperous," rather than "I want to be prosperous." The combination of "I" plus the next word is a powerful expression of intent. So if you say, "I am prosperous," you create the experience of being, not simply wanting. After expressing your intent aloud or in writing, end with gratitude.

As much as you can, remove "should" and "could" from your vocabulary and accept what the energy brings. Sometimes changes are subtle and occur over time. Sometimes they're spectacular and immediate. Sometimes they kick up dust to remove things that aren't serving you before what meets your greatest good arrives. All are normal when working with crystals. Set your intention, do the work, remove judgment and expectation, and allow. The energy will always ultimately serve your highest good.

Storing Crystals

As I mentioned, I have crystals all over my house. Several larger pieces are on display, placed safely on sturdy shelves. I also have some of my more robust small crystals in bowls. The more delicate crystals, however, I store carefully. A multicompartment plastic container, such as one meant to hold beads, is an excellent way to store smaller crystals. If you store them together in a container without compartments, wrap each crystal in a small amount of tissue paper or cloth, and store them away from humidity. Some crystals also lose color when exposed to sunlight, so you may wish to store them away from light, or if you have them on display, keep them away from a sunny window. Such crystals include:

- Amethyst
- Aquamarine
- Aventurine
- Citrine
- Fluorite
- Quartz (any color)
- Sapphire

Crystal Safety

In general, working with crystals is relatively safe. However, some crystals contain substances (such as aluminum, copper, sulfur, fluorine, strontium, or asbestos) that are toxic to humans, so do not put them in the bathtub or make a crystal elixir with them. It's also best to wash your hands when you've finished holding them. These crystals include:

- Aquamarine (contains aluminum)
- Black tourmaline (contains aluminum)
- Celestite (contains strontium)
- Cinnabar (contains mercury)
- Dioptase (contains copper)
- Emerald (contains aluminum)
- Fluorite (contains fluorine)
- Garnet (contains aluminum)
- Iolite (contains aluminum)
- Jade (may contain asbestos)

- Kansas pop rocks (contains aluminum)
- Labradorite (contains aluminum)
- Lapis lazuli (contains pyrite, which contains sulfur)
- Malachite (contains copper)
- Moldavite (contains aluminum)
- Moonstone (contains aluminum)
- Prehnite (contains aluminum)
- Ruby (contains aluminum)
- Sapphire (contains aluminum)
- Sodalite (contains aluminum)
- Spinel (contains aluminum)
- Sugilite (contains aluminum)
- Sulfur (poisonous)
- Tanzanite (contains aluminum)
- Tigers eye, unpolished (contains asbestos)
- Topaz (contains aluminum)
- Tourmaline (contains aluminum)
- Turquoise (contains aluminum)
- Zircon (contains zirconium)

Note that most of the crystals listed above are in this book. For crystals not in the book or on this list, do a little research before you consume an elixir made with them, and wash your hands after handling them, just as a matter of safety.

With the information in this chapter, you can easily get started working with the crystals you already have. The next chapter covers a few advanced concepts for working with crystals that you can use to deepen your practice if you wish. Although learning more isn't necessary, it will provide a few more tools for your toolbox.

CHAPTER
4

MAXIMIZING THE POWER *of* CRYSTALS

Crystals are one form of energy healing, and because they are such a concrete example—something you can actually hold in your hand and use—many people start with crystals and move on to other modalities. Crystals were what started my energy-healing journey.

As an energy healer, I use multiple modalities along with crystals, including chakra work, color and sound practices, meditation and mantras, and more. You can choose to try any of these as you wish. I offer the following information as a way to include more practices in your life, but it's up to you to decide if any resonate with you.

If what you've learned about crystals excites and/or interests you, there are many ways to deepen your understanding and practice of energy healing. Using a single crystal is powerful. Using it in conjunction with other crystals or energy healing modalities can provide even more profound energetic changes in your life.

Crystal Grids

When you purposefully combine crystals with intention and sacred geometry, their energy becomes even more powerful and focused. This is what you are doing when you create a crystal grid. A crystal grid is simply an arrangement of multiple crystals with the intention of creating powerful energy focused on a specific intent.

Grids can be simple or extremely complex. To use a grid, create it anywhere it will be beneficial, such as under your bed or on your desk. Let's take a look at some basic grid shapes, and then we'll discuss two simple grids you can create.

GRID SHAPES

While you can make your grid in any shape, using basic sacred geometric figures can enhance the power.

* Spirals represent the path to consciousness.

* Circles are a representation of oneness and unity.

* *Vesica piscis* (see the figure) represents creation.

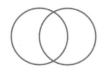

* Squares represent earthly elements.

* Triangles represent the connection between body, mind, and spirit.

GRID ARRANGEMENTS

Grid arrangements use the following elements:

* The focus stone is at the center of the grid. This is the primary energy you are trying to achieve.

- Surrounding stones amplify the energy, allowing it to move outward from the focus.

- Outer stones (not required) can either be the source of intention for the primary energy, or they can be a perimeter stone to keep the energy within the grid.

GRID ONE: FORGIVENESS

Configuration: Spiral
Focus stone: Selenite (any shape)
Perimeter stones (amplify): Clear quartz points

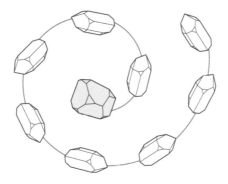

GRID TWO: CREATIVITY

Configuration: Vesica piscis
Focus stone (center): Citrine (any shape)
Perimeter stones: Amethyst (any shape)

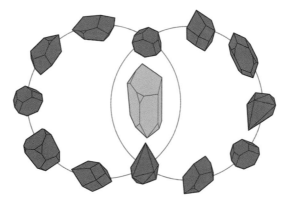

Chakras and Colors

Chakras are energy centers that connect your physical expression to the nonphysical. In other words, they connect your body to the energy of your mind and spirit. Your seven main chakras run along your spinal column. Each expresses a color that corresponds to various energies. Imbalances in the chakras may correspond to physical, emotional, mental, or spiritual issues. To help you balance the energies, you can work with crystals by placing similarly colored crystals on the corresponding chakras.

ROOT Located at the base of your spine, your first or root chakra vibrates red. It's the center of family and tribal (community) identity and relates to safety and security issues, as well as issues of the legs and feet.

SACRAL Your second chakra, which vibrates orange, sits at your belly button. It's the source of prosperity, personal power, and creativity. Digestive, lower back, abdominal, and sexual organ issues are often related to the sacral chakra.

SOLAR PLEXUS Your third chakra vibrates yellow. Located right below your sternum, it's related to self-esteem and boundaries. Physical issues are often related to the lower part of the mid-back, as well as the pancreas and urinary system.

HEART The fourth chakra is located in the center of your chest and vibrates green. It's related to compassion, kindness, unconditional love, and forgiveness. Physical issues may include ribs, lungs, and heart.

THROAT The fifth chakra vibrates blue and is located above your Adam's apple. It's related to speaking your truth and surrendering personal will to Divine guidance. Physical issues include thyroid, throat, and mouth.

THIRD EYE Located in the center of your forehead, the sixth chakra vibrates indigo and corresponds to intuition and intellect. Physical issues include eyes, ears, head, and brain.

CROWN Located at the top of your head, the seventh chakra vibrates white and corresponds with your higher self and Divinity. Systemic issues and musculoskeletal issues are related to the crown chakra.

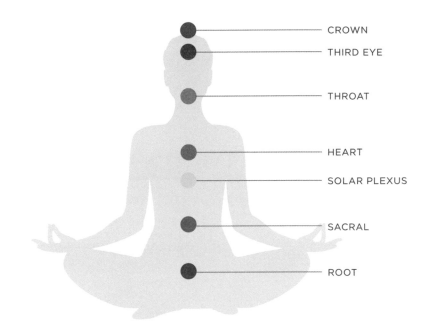

COLOR CORRESPONDENCE

As noted, you'll see that certain issues correspond with the chakras, and each chakra has a different color. Other energies are also associated with colors, so choosing crystals of those colors can help you work through particular issues. The tables on the next two pages offer basic color correspondence for physical, mental, emotional, and spiritual issues.

BLACK / GRAY

PROTECTION • GROUNDING • SAFETY • SECURITY

ISSUES IN THE COMMUNITY (RELATED TO TRIBAL IDENTITY)

UNCONSCIOUS • UNKNOWN • SHADOW SELF

BLUE

TRUTH • WISDOM • LOYALTY • LISTENING

THROAT • THYROID • DENTAL ISSUES • SELF-EXPRESSION

SURRENDERING TO DIVINE WILL

BROWN

WORLDLINESS • EARTH • NATURE • GROUNDING

GREEN

LOVE • HEART • FINANCIAL • WEALTH • FORGIVENESS

COMPASSION • KINDNESS • LUNG ISSUES • PHYSICAL HEALTH

CHANGE • GROWTH

ORANGE / PEACH

FAMILY ISSUES • PERSONAL INTEGRITY • SOCIAL ADAPTATION

SOCIAL ANXIETY • SEXUALITY • SELF-IDENTIFICATION • EGO

LOWER BACK ISSUES • SEXUAL ORGAN ISSUES

PINK

COMPASSION • KINDNESS • FORGIVENESS

UNCONDITIONAL LOVE • ROMANTIC LOVE

RED

PASSION • GROUNDING • PHYSICAL VITALITY AND ENERGY

STAMINA • STABILITY

PURPLE

SPIRITUALITY • DIVINITY • INTUITION

CONNECTION TO HIGHER SELF • INTELLECT • REASON

HEALING • LOYALTY • DEVOTION

MIGRAINES AND HEADACHES • EYE PROBLEMS

WHITE/CLEAR

NEW BEGINNINGS   DIVINITY   PURITY   PEACE

CONNECTION TO HIGHER REALMS

YELLOW / GOLD

SELF-WORTH • SELF-ESTEEM • SELF-LOVE • SELF-IDENTITY

SPIRITUAL RICHNESS • SPLEEN • GALLBLADDER

Meditation and Mantras

The idea of meditating can be daunting for many people because it sounds too difficult to sit quietly and think of nothing. I used to believe the only way to meditate was to sit in the lotus position on the floor chanting "om," which didn't appeal to me. While that is one type of meditation, it's far from the only one. Meditation is anything that focuses your mind on the present moment, and a mantra is any word or phrase that focuses you on an intention or affirmation.

My favorite form is affirmative meditation, sitting comfortably, focused on an object and repeating an affirmation as my mantra. Speaking the affirmations allows me to focus my mind. You can also chant any other mantra that has meaning to you, such as "peace," "joy," "healing," "love," or anything else you'd like to focus on. When you do this holding or gazing at a crystal (which helps you focus even more), you increase the power of the energy and intention.

Focus can be difficult in meditation, so using a mantra or affirmation as well as a crystal can make the practice more accessible and enjoyable. I recommend meditating daily, starting with five minutes and working your way up to 20 minutes or more as you see fit.

In this chapter, I've given you a glimpse of various practices you can use to deepen your work with crystals. Each of these topics is really a book (or at least a chapter) by itself, and there's a lot to explore if you so choose, but they aren't requirements for working with crystals. These are supplementary activities, so feel free to take or leave any of the information as you wish. Working with crystals alone is powerful enough to help you begin to bring positive changes into your life.

Sound Vibration

One of my favorite forms of energy healing to use with crystals is sound healing. Sound vibrates at frequencies, just as colors and crystals do, and those frequencies correspond to different healing energies and chakras. Working with sound by playing a singing bowl (a crystal or metal bowl that rings when you strike it or run a mallet around its rim), listening to Solfeggio frequencies (sacred tones) online or on your smartphone, listening to any type of music, or toning (vocalizing) notes and sounds with your voice all increase the power of intent and amplify crystal energy. You can also use sound to cleanse crystals as described on page 33.

You don't have to go out and buy singing bowls to work with sound. A quick online search shows there are abundant recordings of people playing singing bowls to correspond to different chakras. I'll also list a few sound resources for you in the resources section on page 182 in case this is something you'd like to explore further.

You can also vocalize various vowel sounds for a minute or two each in meditation to affect the vibrations of each chakra.

ROOT—*Uhhhhhhh* (as in bug)

SACRAL—*Oooooo* (as in too)

SOLAR PLEXUS—*Ohhhh* (as in so)

HEART—*Ahh* (as in saw)

THROAT—*Eye* (as in my)

THIRD EYE—*Ay* (as in day)

CROWN—*Eeeeee* (as in see)

PART
2

Deepen Your Knowledge of Crystals

CHAPTER

5

10 CRYSTALS
for EVERYONE

While my list of favorite crystals shifts as my life issues and energetic needs change, there are certain crystals I always recommend, especially for people just getting started. I have all of these crystals and often buy them in bulk to keep with me so I can share them. It makes my purse a little heavy, but I enjoy sharing the power of these basic crystals so others can benefit.

These are the workhorse crystals you can use for multiple issues. They are also relatively easy to find—most metaphysical and crystal shops stock a large supply of all of these stones, and the crystals are durable and inexpensive. Choose any form of the crystal that appeals to you in a size and shape that pleases you. What truly matters here are the basic properties of the crystals as opposed to the size, shape, or condition of the stones.

AMETHYST

Amethyst is a form of quartz. The most common color is purple, although you can also find heat-treated versions that are green (prasiolite) and yellow (so-called "citrine," see page 60). The word amethyst comes from the Greek amethystos, *meaning "not drunken," which speaks to the traditional use of amethyst as a stone to prevent drunkenness. It also brings safety to travelers and is related to the third eye, which is the seat of intuition. Many use the stone for other issues as well, such as transmuting negativity or assisting with insomnia and dreams, making this a valuable all-purpose stone.*

ORIGIN: Brazil, Germany, Sri Lanka, Uruguay

LATTICE: Hexagonal

SHAPES: Natural, points, clusters, geodes, tumbled/polished, cut

ENERGY: Amplifies

COLORS: Violet to deep purple, green (heat-treated, prasiolite), yellow (heat-treated, "citrine")

CHAKRA: Third eye, crown

PLACEMENT: On third eye chakra, above crown of head, near your bed, under a pillow

HELPS WITH: Intuition and insight, insomnia, safe travel, connecting to higher self and the Divine, creativity, manifestation, stress and anxiety, nightmares, addiction

WORKS WITH: Citrine, clear quartz

USAGE TIP: Tape to the bottom side of the head of your bed or put it on your bedside table to help fight insomnia and to ward off nightmares and/or help you remember your dreams.

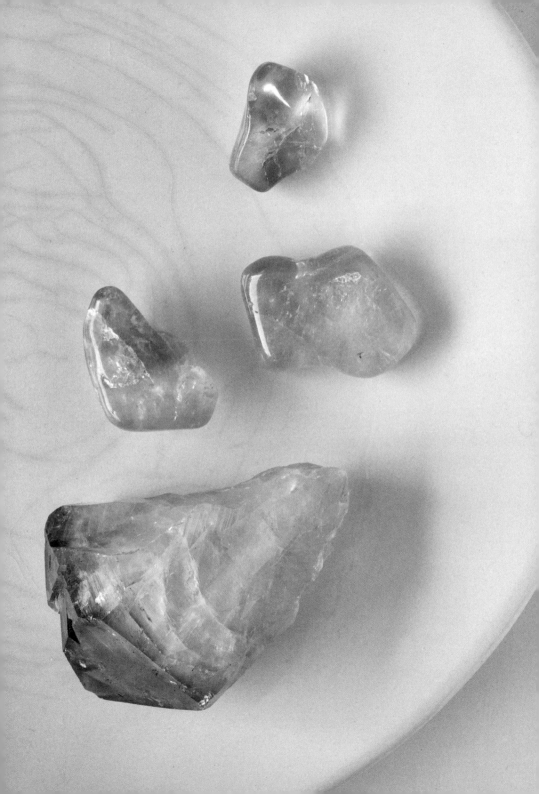

BLACK TOURMALINE

I carry black tourmaline (also known as schorl) with me at all times both to give to others and to help absorb any negativity that comes from around me. In ancient times, magicians used black tourmaline to ward off "demons." Along with absorbing negativity and providing protection, black tourmaline also helps keep you grounded, and it promotes self-confidence and can help purify environments where a lot of emotional negativity has occurred. If a piece of black tourmaline breaks, it has become saturated with the negative energy it has absorbed. Discard it (just return it to the Earth), and get a new piece.

ORIGIN: Australia, Brazil, Sri Lanka, United States

LATTICE: Hexagonal

SHAPES: Natural, in quartz, tumbled/polished, cut

ENERGY: Absorbs

COLORS: Black

CHAKRA: Root

PLACEMENT: Pants pocket, near root chakra, next to the bed, between you and a source of negativity

HELPS WITH: Psychic protection, protection against negativity, grounding, stress release, cleansing negative emotions

WORKS WITH: Clear quartz

USAGE TIP: If you have an excessively negative coworker, position a piece of black tourmaline between you and that person.

CARNELIAN

Carnelian is a variety of chalcedony, which is in the quartz family. Carnelian is associated with boldness and courage, and using this crystal can help strengthen weaknesses (physical and emotional), improve luck, and attract prosperity. As a stone of the sacral chakra, carnelian can also help strengthen your sense of self as well as temper excessive ego. Traditionally, carnelian has also been used to help vocalists and public speakers by bringing strength and power to the voice.

ORIGIN: Brazil, Iceland, India, Peru

LATTICE: Hexagonal

SHAPES: Natural, tumbled/polished, cut

ENERGY: Absorbs

COLORS: Brownish-orange to red-orange

CHAKRA: Red-orange—root; orange, brown-orange—sacral

PLACEMENT: On or near your belly button, as a bracelet, near the root chakra

HELPS WITH: Courage, security and safety, willpower, determination, returning passion to relationships, developing a healthy sense of self, focusing on the present moment, overcoming abuse, protection against envy, boosting energy

WORKS WITH: Clear quartz, malachite, sardonyx

USAGE TIP: Boost your energy by wearing this crystal when you work out, or keep a piece at your desk at work to help maintain energy throughout the day. Since carnelian boosts energy, you probably don't want to keep it near your bed.

CITRINE

I have citrine strategically located all around my house, both because it is so beautiful and because it is a powerful stone. You can find two types of citrine: naturally occurring citrine and citrine that has been created by heat-treating amethyst. In general, if the golden yellow color of citrine is extremely clear and saturated, it means it is heat-treated amethyst. If you're unsure, ask before you buy. While the heat-treated amethyst has similar properties to naturally occurring citrine, the naturally occurring form tends to have more powerful energy.

ORIGIN: Brazil, Peru, Russia, United States

LATTICE: Hexagonal

SHAPES: Natural, clusters, in clear quartz, tumbled/polished, cut

ENERGY: Amplifies

COLORS: Yellow

CHAKRA: Solar plexus

PLACEMENT: On or near your solar plexus; as a bracelet, ring, or necklace; in your cashbox or wallet; in the back left corner of your home (the prosperity corner)

HELPS WITH: Prosperity, self-esteem and self-image, creativity, encouraging generosity, promoting clarity of thinking, manifestation, asserting personal will, facilitating new beginnings

WORKS WITH: Clear quartz, amethyst, ametrine, smoky quartz

USAGE TIP: To enhance prosperity, place citrine in the back left corner of your home (the prosperity corner). You can determine the back left corner by standing at the front door and facing inward. You can also place it in the back left corner of any room to enhance prosperity. If you run a business, place it in your cash register or cash box to promote prosperity for the business.

CLEAR QUARTZ

Clear quartz is, hands down, the most versatile crystal in any collection. It's always the first crystal I recommend to people, and one of the crystals I always carry with me in bulk to give to others. It is a self-cleansing crystal, and you can use it to cleanse other crystals if you have a large cluster of it. Clear quartz amplifies the power of any crystal it works with. You can use points of clear quartz to direct and amplify the energy of another stone by placing the flat end of the quartz at the crystal and the point away from it.

ORIGIN: All over the world

LATTICE: Hexagonal

SHAPES: Natural, points, double-terminated points (Herkimer diamonds), clusters, geodes, tumbled/polished, cut

ENERGY: Amplifies

COLORS: Milky white to clear

CHAKRA: Crown, all other chakras

PLACEMENT: Anywhere, for meditation on or near crown chakra, in a grid with other crystals to amplify their energies

HELPS WITH: Amplifying the properties of all other crystals, connection to the Divine and higher consciousness, working through all conditions (master healer), protection, cleansing and purification, amplifying energy and thought, clarifying thoughts and beliefs, balancing body-mind-spirit, improving concentration

WORKS WITH: All other crystals

USAGE TIP: Use a cluster of clear quartz points to cleanse other stones safely and effectively. Place smaller stones in the cluster and allow them to sit for 12 to 24 hours.

FLUORITE

Part of the versatility of fluorite is the range of colors it comes in, from light green to the deepest of purples. The most versatile piece of fluorite is rainbow fluorite, which has bands of green, purple, pink, blue, and aqua throughout, so it works with several chakras and embodies the healing properties of its various colors. Rainbow fluorite facilitates energy flow among your chakras and helps promote clarity and clear thinking. It's a relatively soft mineral, so be careful how you store it because it scratches easily.

ORIGIN: Australia, Brazil, China, United States

LATTICE: Isometric

SHAPES: Natural, clusters, geodes, tumbled/polished, cut

ENERGY: Absorbs

COLORS: Aqua, blue, clear, green, pink, purple, rainbow, yellow

CHAKRA: Heart, throat, third eye, crown

PLACEMENT: Anywhere along the four upper chakras, as a necklace

HELPS WITH: Balancing and stabilizing energies, body-mind-spirit connection, facilitating intuition and communication with higher planes, calming, enhancing creativity, harmonizing, connection to the Divine

WORKS WITH: Clear quartz, amethyst, sodalite

USAGE TIP: Store away from other crystals as it scratches easily. Hold fluorite while meditating to focus on balancing energies.

HEMATITE

Hematite is a really pretty stone. It's shiny and black with a rainbow of colors along the surface, like an oil slick on water when the sunlight hits it. This is a stone that absorbs energies, making it perfect for when there's a lot of negative energy around. It is also grounding and calming, so it's a great stone for when you are stressed out. Hematite also helps you release limitations you've created for yourself without realizing you've done so.

ORIGIN: Brazil, Switzerland, United Kingdom

LATTICE: Hexagonal

SHAPES: Natural, tumbled/polished, cut, rings

ENERGY: Absorbs

COLORS: Dark gray/black

CHAKRA: Root

PLACEMENT: Near the root chakra, wear it as a ring or bracelet, in a pocket, at your desk for a stressful job

HELPS WITH: Absorbing negativity, balancing energies, relieving stress and anxiety, grounding, detoxifying

WORKS WITH: Lapis lazuli, malachite

USAGE TIP: Hematite absorbs a lot of negative energies and it's constantly at work. Because of this, it often breaks. When it breaks, return it to the Earth and get a new piece.

ROSE QUARTZ

Rose quartz is the stone of unconditional love, kindness, and compassion. As such, it can help with forgiveness as well. Although the heart chakra is green in color, pink stones like rose quartz are deeply associated with this chakra, too. This is a wonderful stone for self-healing, especially when you're trying to heal love-based emotional upsets such as the breakup of a relationship, betrayal, or the loss of a loved one. This is a calm, peaceful stone that can help you feel connected to others and strengthen your sensation of joy.

ORIGIN: Brazil, India, Japan, United States

LATTICE: Hexagonal

SHAPES: Natural, points, clusters, tumbled/polished, cut

ENERGY: Amplifies

COLORS: Pink

CHAKRA: Heart

PLACEMENT: As a necklace, bracelet, or ring (particularly on your commitment or ring finger); near or on the heart chakra

HELPS WITH: Compassion, kindness, unconditional love, self-love, emotional healing, joy, peace, playfulness

WORKS WITH: Clear quartz, amethyst, prasiolite, peridot

USAGE TIP: Carry rose quartz with you after an argument with a loved one to help facilitate healing.

SMOKY QUARTZ

*Smoky quartz is another of my go-to stones because it transmutes nega-
tivity into positivity. I use smoky quartz when people want me to balance
the energy of their home, and I always carry it with me because its effects
on energy are so powerful. When a friend's business was flooded recently,
there was a lot of negativity associated with the event, so once cleanup had
occurred, I sprinkled chips of smoky quartz all around the business prem-
ises to help cleanse the associated negativity.*

ORIGIN: All over the world

LATTICE: Hexagonal

SHAPES: Natural, points, clusters,
tumbled/polished, cut

ENERGY: Amplifies

COLORS: Light gray to brown

CHAKRA: Root, crown

PLACEMENT: In your pocket,
near your root chakra *and* your
crown chakra, anywhere you feel
negative energy is an issue

HELPS WITH: Transmuting
negative energy to positive energy,
amplifying positive energy, grounding, detoxifying, connecting all
the chakras to balance energies,
connection to higher guidance and
the Divine

WORKS WITH: Clear quartz,
citrine, amethyst

USAGE TIP: Sprinkle chips of
smoky quartz all around the perimeter of your house (and, if you buy
enough, around the perimeter of
your property) so that all the energy
that surrounds where you live is
changed into positive energy. I do
this for myself, and also for friends
who move into new homes to bring
good energy.

TURQUOISE

Turquoise has deep symbolism for many nations and aboriginal tribes. Historically, it was a stone of shamans and warriors. Its use as a sacred stone is ancient and worldwide. One traditional belief is that turquoise protects riders from falls. Others prize it for its ability to promote clear vision, spirituality, and personal and spiritual power. One note of caution—make sure you are purchasing real turquoise. Many vendors sell dyed howlite, which has similar veining as turquoise and can easily pass for the stone.

ORIGIN: All over the world

LATTICE: Triclinic

SHAPES: Natural, points, tumbled/polished, cut

ENERGY: Absorbs

COLORS: Light blue to deep turquoise

CHAKRA: Throat

PLACEMENT: In jewelry, particularly as a necklace; on throat chakra during meditation; in a pocket, particularly a chest pocket

HELPS WITH: Personal power, luck and prosperity, safe travel, speaking personal truth, giving voice to creative ideas, protection against theft, promoting ambition and empowerment, calming, absorbing excessive energy, harmonizing

WORKS WITH: Clear quartz, onyx

USAGE TIP: If your relationship is struggling, place turquoise in your bedroom to promote harmony.

CHAPTER
6

40 CRYSTALS
to KNOW

If you walk into a crystal shop, you'll discover a staggering array of crystals, which can seem overwhelming. While I always recommend purchasing crystals you feel drawn to, a little foreknowledge can help you navigate the waters of a crystal shop more easily. In this chapter, you'll find 40 commonly available crystals that are affordable, versatile, and easy to find in metaphysical and crystal stores, so they make great starter crystals that can suit your purposes now and into the future.

As time passes, your crystal needs may change. While this chapter contains some suggestions, as your needs change you may be drawn to different crystals. If crystals that are not in this chapter draw you to them, don't be afraid to choose those that choose you, regardless of what I recommend. Be open to the experience of finding the right crystal for you through the use of your inner guidance.

AGATE

Agates come in a variety of colors—all the colors of the rainbow. Different stones will therefore have slightly differing properties depending on their color. However, since agates are composed of quartz crystals (usually chalcedony), they have a hexagonal structure, which means that in general, agates will help you achieve desires.

ORIGIN: All over the world

LATTICE: Hexagonal

SHAPES: Natural, tumbled/polished, sliced

ENERGY: Amplifies

COLORS: Black, blue, brown, gray, green, multicolored, orange, purple, red, white, yellow

CHAKRA: All depending on color

PLACEMENT: On any chakra, in a pocket, as any type of jewelry

HELPS WITH: Emotional balance, calmness, focus and concentration; blue—communication and honesty; moss—unconditional love, prosperity; orange-brown—self-control; pink—compassion; other colors—issues associated with the chakras of the same color

WORKS WITH: Other agates, clear quartz

USAGE TIP: I spent a lot of time as a kid on rocky beaches searching for agates. To find them, sift through the rocks and hold the stones up to the sunlight to see if the sun shines through. If it does, it's an agate.

AMAZONITE

A variety of feldspar, amazonite is known as the Stone of Truth and the Stone of Courage. Its blue-green color aligns it with both the heart and the throat chakras. With shades reminiscent of the ocean, it promotes tranquility and peace. It is also a balancing stone.

ORIGIN: Australia, Brazil, Canada, United States

LATTICE: Monoclinic

SHAPES: Natural, tumbled/polished

ENERGY: Absorbs

COLORS: Aqua, blue-green, green

CHAKRA: Heart, throat

PLACEMENT: On the heart chakra or throat chakra, or between the two; as a necklace or earrings

HELPS WITH: Speaking the truth, balancing between throat and heart chakras, loving unconditionally, peace and understanding, integrity, forgiveness, prosperity, protecting against negative emotions

WORKS WITH: Rose quartz

USAGE TIP: Wear amazonite as a necklace or bracelet the next time you have a stressful day coming up— it will help calm you.

AMBER

Amber is not technically a crystal—it's petrified tree sap. However, many people use it like a crystal because it has healing properties. It is best known in alternative health care as an anti-inflammatory used in baby teething necklaces (they wear it while supervised and don't actually chew on it).

ORIGIN: Baltic countries, Germany, Romania, Russia

LATTICE: Amorphous

SHAPES: Natural, cut

ENERGY: Absorbs and amplifies

COLORS: Brown, gold, golden-brown, honey, orange

CHAKRA: Solar plexus

PLACEMENT: On the solar plexus chakra, near any area of pain or inflammation, as jewelry, in a pocket

HELPS WITH: Pain and inflammation, generating positive energy, self-esteem, cleansing, stress relief, increasing life force, relieving anxiety, warding off others' energy (excellent for empathic people)

WORKS WITH: By itself it's quite powerful, but it works well in conjunction with clear quartz.

USAGE TIP: For arthritis-related pain in the hands, try wearing an amber bracelet.

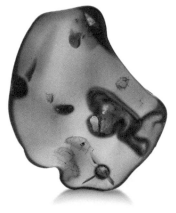

AMETRINE

In ametrine, citrine and amethyst naturally form in a single crystal. With the purple and yellow in the crystal, it is exceptionally beautiful, and it combines and amplifies the properties of each crystal to make a whole. From a pure beauty standpoint, it is one of my favorites.

ORIGIN: Canada, Mexico, Sri Lanka, United States

LATTICE: Hexagonal

SHAPES: Natural, points, clusters, tumbled/polished, cut

ENERGY: Amplifies

COLORS: Yellow and purple

CHAKRA: Solar plexus, third eye, crown

PLACEMENT: On the solar plexus or third eye chakra, near the crown of the head, near the head of your bed

HELPS WITH: Amplifying the properties of both citrine and amethyst, prosperity and abundance, psychic communication, aura cleansing, transmuting negativity, facilitating positive energy flow, balancing opposing energies, balancing Divine will with personal will, raising ego-based thought to a higher level, promoting spiritual dreaming

WORKS WITH: Amethyst, citrine, clear quartz

USAGE TIP: Wearing an ametrine necklace can help facilitate and balance the flow of the energy from the solar plexus through the crown chakras.

APACHE TEARS

Apache tears are obsidian stones in a rounded or oval shape. They aren't technically crystals but rather a form of volcanic glass. However, they do have healing properties, particularly for people who are grieving.

ORIGIN: All over the world

LATTICE: Amorphous

SHAPES: Natural—oval or round

ENERGY: Absorbs

COLORS: Dark gray to black

CHAKRA: Root

PLACEMENT: In your pocket when dealing with negative emotions, as a worry stone in your giving (dominant) hand

HELPS WITH: Grief, emotional healing, recovery from dark or sad emotions

WORKS WITH: Rose quartz

USAGE TIP: When dealing with the death of a loved one, carry Apache tears with you and use them as a worry stone when grief threatens to overwhelm you.

APATITE

Apatite has a beautiful blue-green color, but it's also a rather brittle, soft stone. Don't store apatite with other crystals. Instead, store it carefully wrapped to keep it from becoming damaged. This stone is associated deeply with spiritual wisdom and truth.

ORIGIN: Mexico, Norway, Russia, United States

LATTICE: Hexagonal

SHAPES: Natural, points, tumbled/polished, cut

ENERGY: Amplifies

COLORS: Aqua, blue, violet, yellow

CHAKRA: Pink—heart or root, yellow—solar plexus, aqua—heart, blue or aqua—throat, violet—third eye, clear—crown

PLACEMENT: On the chakra that corresponds with its color, in a pocket (carefully wrapped) when you're feeling socially anxious, in your receiving (nondominant) hand while meditating

HELPS WITH: Focusing on goals, connecting to the Divine, eliminating negativity, raising energetic vibration, enhancing intuition, fascilitating truth, motivation, decreasing social anxiety and self-consciousness

WORKS WITH: Amethyst, clear quartz, rose quartz

USAGE TIP: Use caution when storing apatite, as it scratches, cracks, and chips easily.

AQUAMARINE

Aquamarine is a manifestation stone. Its beautiful blue-green color is calming and soothing, so it's an especially useful stone for people with anxiety or phobias; it is also a travel protection stone.

ORIGIN: Brazil, Mexico, Russia, United States

LATTICE: Hexagonal

SHAPES: Natural, points, tumbled/polished, cut

ENERGY: Amplifies

COLORS: Blue, green-blue

CHAKRA: Heart, throat, third eye

PLACEMENT: On throat chakra to balance energy flowing from heart to third eye chakra, as a necklace, as any type of aquamarine jewelry (particularly earrings) to help with anxiety and phobias, in your receiving (nondominant) hand while meditating and/or speaking affirmations

HELPS WITH: Calming, soothing anxiety, easing phobias, assisting with manifestation, aligning and balancing chakras, and promoting courage, protection, self-expression, and the discovery of spiritual truth

WORKS WITH: Amethyst, clear quartz, turquoise

USAGE TIP: When you speak your affirmations, hold aquamarine in your receiving (nondominant) hand to help manifestation.

AVENTURINE

Formed from quartz with inclusions of other minerals (which cause different colors), aventurine may be blue, green, red, orange, yellow, or white although green is the most common. With quartz as its main component, aventurine is an energy amplifier that can amplify chakra energies associated with the color of the stone.

ORIGIN: Brazil, China, Russia, Tibet

LATTICE: Hexagonal

SHAPES: Natural, points, tumbled/polished, cut

ENERGY: Amplifies

COLORS: Blue, blue-green, green (most common), red, orange, yellow, white

CHAKRA: Red—root, orange—sacral, green—heart, yellow—solar plexus, blue—third eye and throat, white—crown

PLACEMENT: On the corresponding chakra, as jewelry, in your wallet

HELPS WITH: Blue—enhancing communication, aiding in manifestation, improving self-discipline; green—enhancing leadership abilities, promoting prosperity, promoting unconditional love, releases anxiety; red/orange—promoting a sense of safety and security; white—enhancing communication with higher self, balancing chakras; yellow—promoting self-esteem

WORKS WITH: Tourmaline, turquoise

USAGE TIP: Carry a piece of green aventurine in your pocket when you have an important meeting coming up at work, to promote leadership.

CALCITE

Calcite comes in a rainbow of colors, each with specific properties associated with the chakras with which they align. Its hexagonal structure means that calcite is a stone to help you achieve your desires, so it's excellent for manifestation work.

ORIGIN: Brazil, Iceland, Russia, United States

LATTICE: Hexagonal

SHAPES: Natural, tumbled/polished, cut

ENERGY: Amplifies

COLORS: Black, blue, gray, green, honey, orange/peach, pink, red, violet, white

CHAKRA: Red, black, or gray—root: orange or peach—sacral; honey or yellow—solar plexus; green or pink—heart; blue—throat; violet—third eye; white—crown

PLACEMENT: On the corresponding chakra, in a pocket, in your receiving (nondominant) hand while meditating

HELPS WITH: Manifestation, energy amplification, cleansing, grounding, inner peace; blue—recognizing and speaking your truth, integrity; green—abundance; green/pink—unconditional love; honey or yellow—self-esteem; purple—intuition; orange—personal will; white—communicating with a higher power, spiritual growth

WORKS WITH: Other calcites in different colors

USAGE TIP: Create a peaceful and relaxing environment in a bedroom or bathroom by placing different colored calcite stones around the room.

CHALCEDONY

Chalcedony is a form of quartz that gets its color from mineral occlusions. Agates are a form of chalcedony (as is carnelian); however, when discussing healing crystals, chalcedony typically refers to a creamy-blue variety of the stone. Known as the Speaker's Stone, it helps you speak your truth with tact.

ORIGIN: Austria, Brazil, Russia, United States

LATTICE: Hexagonal/monoclinic

SHAPES: Natural, geode, tumbled/polished, cut

ENERGY: Amplifies

COLORS: Blue

CHAKRA: Throat

PLACEMENT: In necklaces and earrings (works especially well), directly on the throat chakra, in a chest pocket

HELPS WITH: Manifestation, protection, expressing your truth, expressing creative ideas, promoting peace, lessening self-doubt, balancing emotions

WORKS WITH: Clear quartz, sodalite, lapis lazuli

USAGE TIP: Touch chalcedony to the tip of your tongue or to your lips before public speaking.

DANBURITE

Danburite comes in multiple colors that affect different chakras. However, all colors are high-vibration stones associated with spiritual enlightenment and connection to a higher power. It is also a cleansing and clearing stone that can help heal deep emotional pain and wounds.

ORIGIN: Japan, Mexico, Russia, United States

LATTICE: Orthorhombic

SHAPES: Natural, tumbled/polished

ENERGY: Amplifies

COLORS: Clear, gray, green

CHAKRA: Green—heart, clear and gray—crown

PLACEMENT: On the heart or crown chakra, in a pocket during times of stress, around the home to promote healing energy throughout

HELPS WITH: Intuition, deep emotional healing, compassion and unconditional love, connecting the upper chakras (heart through crown), easing transitions, calming and de-stressing, purifying the aura, cleansing

WORKS WITH: All crystals, particularly high-vibration synergy stones like phenacite, tektite, and moldavite

USAGE TIP: Danburite is an excellent meditation stone when you wish to connect with your higher power. Hold it in either hand as you meditate.

EMERALD

Often cut and polished and made into jewelry, emerald is one form of a mineral called beryl. Other beryls include aquamarine and morganite. With its characteristic green color, emerald is a classic heart chakra stone that promotes love and compassion.

ORIGIN: Austria, Brazil, Tanzania, Zimbabwe

LATTICE: Hexagonal

SHAPES: Natural, tumbled/polished, cut

ENERGY: Amplifies

COLORS: Green

CHAKRA: Heart

PLACEMENT: On the heart chakra, as jewelry, as a ring on the commitment (ring) finger.

HELPS WITH: Prosperity, unconditional love, compassion, romance, kindness, forgiveness, manifestation, increasing spiritual awareness, serenity, experiencing Divine love, protection, healing trauma

WORKS WITH: Other beryls (aquamarine, morganite), clear quartz, other green or pink stones

USAGE TIP: As a stone of unconditional and romantic love, emerald is especially auspicious to give to another person as a promise, engagement, or wedding ring stone. Emerald is a hard stone but has lots of inclusions, so they break easily, which means you need to be especially careful with them.

EPIDOTE

As a monoclinic stone, epidote is a protective stone primarily associated with the heart chakra and love. It can help improve interpersonal relationships, creating balance between partners and enhancing love and personal growth. It also amplifies the energy of other stones.

ORIGIN: Canada, France, Norway, Russia, United States

LATTICE: Monoclinic

SHAPES: Natural, tumbled/polished

ENERGY: Amplifies

COLORS: Green

CHAKRA: Heart

PLACEMENT: On the heart chakra, in the hand after meditation for a grounding effect, next to any stone where you wish amplification to occur

HELPS WITH: Prosperity, love, connection with nature, optimism, grounding, clearing energetic blockages, clearing ruts, strengthening, stimulating healing

WORKS WITH: Any stone that needs amplification

USAGE TIP: If you live in a city and haven't been able to get out much, meditate with epidote to help you connect with the natural world.

FUCHSITE

Fuchsite is a sparkling green silicate mineral embedded with mica. The stone is protective. Often, you will find fuchsite embedded with ruby. Fuchsite (with or without ruby) is a classic healer's stone that can help with physical, energetic, and emotional healing.

ORIGIN: Brazil, India, Russia

LATTICE: Monoclinic

SHAPES: Natural, tumbled/polished

ENERGY: Absorbs

COLORS: Green

CHAKRA: Heart

PLACEMENT: On the heart chakra; if embedded with ruby, on root chakra and heart chakra; as a necklace or bracelet

HELPS WITH: Emotional-physical-spiritual healing, renewal, rejuvenation, balance, prosperity, love, intensifying energy of other crystals

WORKS WITH: Ruby

USAGE TIP: Fuchsite is a soft mineral that easily gets dings in it, so store it away from other crystals.

GARNET

When people think of garnets, they most commonly think of red garnets, called pyrope. However, garnets are available in other colors, as well. For example, spessartine garnets are yellow to orange, and tsavorite garnets are green.

ORIGIN: All over the world

LATTICE: Isometric

SHAPES: Natural, points, clusters, tumbled/polished, cut

ENERGY: Amplifies

COLORS: Brown, green, orange-red, red, yellow

CHAKRA: Red—root, orange-red or brown—sacral, green—heart

PLACEMENT: Red near root chakra; orange-red or brown on sacral chakra; green on heart chakra; in jewelry, particularly rings or bracelets

HELPS WITH: Amplification of energies, protection, manifestation, transitions, energizing and revitalizing, boosting energy, overcoming trauma, getting rid of limiting ideas and beliefs; green (tsavorite)—abundance; red—grounding, protection; yellow to orange (spessartine)—career success

WORKS WITH: Garnets of other colors, smoky quartz, clear quartz

USAGE TIP: If you're going through a transition, carry garnet in your pocket or wear it as jewelry to help ease the transition.

HOWLITE

Because it has veins similar to turquoise, howlite is often dyed blue and sold as that gemstone. However, undyed howlite is lightly colored; it's white, gray, or colorless, which is why it is so easily dyed. It is a stone used to link people to the Divine.

ORIGIN: United States

LATTICE: Monoclinic

SHAPES: Natural, tumbled/polished, carved, cut

ENERGY: Absorbs

COLORS: White, gray, colorless

CHAKRA: Crown

PLACEMENT: Near the crown chakra, as earrings or a necklace

HELPS WITH: Attunement to the Divine, connecting to higher truth, calming anxiety, reducing stress, easing extreme negative emotions like rage

WORKS WITH: Turquoise, amethyst, sodalite

USAGE TIP: During times of high stress or tension, wear carved howlite jewelry to help calm you.

JADE

Jade has been used since ancient times, often carved into jewelry or other artifacts. Most people recognize green jade; however, it may also be white or orange. Because it has been popular for so many centuries and is of value in many cultures, there are plenty of manufactured or dyed jade objects. Check for irregularities in color, particularly under magnification, to determine its authenticity. If there are irregularites, it is probably real jade.

ORIGIN: China, Middle East, Russia, United States

LATTICE: Monoclinic

SHAPES: Natural, tumbled/polished, carved

ENERGY: Absorbs

COLORS: Black, blue, gray, green (most common), orange, purple, red, white, yellow

CHAKRA: Red, black, or gray—root; orange—sacral; yellow—solar plexus; blue—throat; green—heart; purple—third eye; white—crown

PLACEMENT: On any of the corresponding chakras, as jewelry, in a pocket

HELPS WITH: Protection, safe travel, easing guilt, interrupting negative thought patterns, reducing excessive thirst for power, strengthening life force energies, increasing trust, promoting love of all kinds

WORKS WITH: All colors of jade, clear quartz, malachite

USAGE TIP: Jade may contain asbestos, so it's best to wash your hands after handling.

JASPER

There are multiple opaque colors and varieties of jasper, which is an aggregate of quartz or chalcedony and other minerals. Different varieties have varying properties. In general, however, jasper is a manifestation stone that absorbs excess energies to help with energetic balance.

ORIGIN: All over the world

LATTICE: Hexagonal

SHAPES: Natural, tumbled/polished, carved, cut

ENERGY: Absorbs

COLORS: Black, blue, brown, green, orange, red, yellow

CHAKRA: Red or black—root, orange—sacral, yellow or brown—solar plexus, green—heart, blue—throat or third eye

PLACEMENT: On any of the corresponding chakras, as jewelry, in a pocket

HELPS WITH: Manifestation, balancing energies of excess (e.g., addiction, obsessive-compulsive behavior), grounding, stability

WORKS WITH: All other jaspers, black tourmaline

USAGE TIP: Hold after meditation and visualize roots going into the Earth from your feet, to help ground you.

KYANITE

While blue is the most common color of kyanite, it also comes in yellow, green, black, and orange. It is a brittle stone that is often blade shaped, which makes it a good worry stone for rubbing your thumb across. Kyanite never needs cleansing because it doesn't hold energy—it just facilitates its movement. This is also why neither absorption nor amplification is noted for this crystal.

ORIGIN: Brazil

LATTICE: Triclinic

SHAPES: Natural, blades, tumbled/polished, carved, cut

COLORS: Black, blue (most common), gray, green, orange, yellow, white

CHAKRA: Black or gray—root, orange—sacral, yellow—solar plexus, green—heart, blue—throat or third eye, white—crown

PLACEMENT: On any of the corresponding chakras, in your hand as a worry stone

HELPS WITH: Creating pathways from one thing to another, clearing blockages, getting you out of a rut, facilitating communication (particularly blue), loyalty and fairness, memory recall, grounding (black)

WORKS WITH: All colors of kyanite, between any two crystals to help facilitate movement of one energy to the other

USAGE TIP: Use kyanite between other crystals in a grid to facilitate energy flow from one crystal to the next.

LABRADORITE

When it's not cut or polished, labradorite just looks like any old rock. However, after cutting and polishing, it has a quality called labradorescence, which is an opalescent sheen of multiple colors similar to that in opals or moonstone. First Nation Inuit people believe labradorite is a connection between the earthly plane and unseen realms.

ORIGIN: Canada, Italy, Scandinavia

LATTICE: Triclinic

SHAPES: Natural, tumbled/polished, carved, cut

ENERGY: Amplifies

COLORS: Blue or gray with multiple flashes of color

CHAKRA: Throat, third eye

PLACEMENT: On the throat chakra, as a necklace, near where you meditate

HELPS WITH: Bringing out magical qualities, reducing negativity, tempering negative aspects of the personality, detoxification of addictive substances, tempering impulsivity and recklessness, connection to higher realms, aiding in intuition, dispelling illusion

WORKS WITH: Clear quartz, sodalite, amethyst

USAGE TIP: Use labradorite (hold it or have it next to you) during meditation or prayer to aid in communication with higher realms.

LAPIS LAZULI

Lapis lazuli isn't technically a crystal, because it doesn't have a crystalline structure. Rather, it is a metamorphic rock. However, it has been prized for centuries as a semiprecious stone having magical powers. It adorns many antiquities, including the sarcophagus of King Tutankhamen.

ORIGIN: Chile, Egypt, Middle East, United States

LATTICE: None

SHAPES: Natural, tumbled/polished, carved

ENERGY: Absorbs

COLORS: Blue with white or gold streaks

CHAKRA: Throat

PLACEMENT: On the throat chakra, as a necklace or earrings

HELPS WITH: Communication of all types (particularly written communication), learning, encouraging honesty and speaking one's truth, bringing harmony, improving performance

WORKS WITH: Clear quartz

USAGE TIP: Lapis lazuli is a performer's stone. Wear it for auditions or public speaking engagements to help facilitate a better performance.

LARIMAR

Larimar is a blue version of the stone pectolite. It is found only in the Dominican Republic. This is a calming, tranquil stone that forms in lava. It is also known as the Dolphin Stone and the Atlantis Stone.

ORIGIN: Dominican Republic

LATTICE: Triclinic

SHAPES: Natural, blades, tumbled/polished, carved

ENERGY: Absorbs

COLORS: Blue

CHAKRA: Throat, third eye

PLACEMENT: On the throat chakra, next to your bed or taped under the head of your bed

HELPS WITH: Relaxation, calming and soothing, promoting peace and serenity, aiding in giving voice to wisdom, assisting in resolving trauma, clarifying meaning of dreams

WORKS WITH: Clear quartz, selenite

USAGE TIP: Wear Larimar as a necklace for conversations when it is important you speak your truth calmly and wisely.

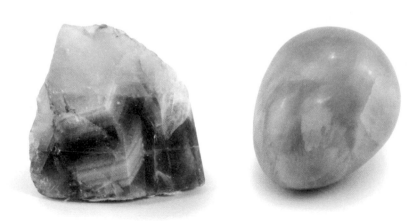

LODESTONE

Lodestone, also called magnetite, is a black magnetic stone made from iron oxide. You can often find it with small pieces of iron stuck to it via magnetism. If you find it this way, store it carefully away from other crystals so it continues to hold on to the small pieces of iron.

ORIGIN: Austria, Canada, Mexico, United States

LATTICE: Monoclinic

SHAPES: Natural, natural with iron stuck to it, tumbled/polished (no iron)

ENERGY: Amplifies

COLORS: Black

CHAKRA: Root

PLACEMENT: Near the root chakra, in a bracelet

HELPS WITH: Grounding, protection, attracting what you create

WORKS WITH: By itself it's quite powerful

USAGE TIP: I recommend always keeping lodestone in a protective container, even when using it.

MALACHITE

Malachite was the first crystal I discovered many years ago—when I was a child. It's a beautiful deep green color with bands of lighter and darker green through it. It is a stone of the heart, nature, prosperity, and healing.

ORIGIN: Congo, Middle East, Russia, Zambia

LATTICE: Monoclinic

SHAPES: Natural, tumbled/polished, carved, cut

ENERGY: Absorbs

COLORS: Green

CHAKRA: Heart

PLACEMENT: On or near the heart chakra, as a necklace or bracelet, in a suitcase or carry-on bag during travel

HELPS WITH: Absorbing negative energy, guarding against pollution (energetic and physical), protecting against accidents, relieving fears associated with travel

WORKS WITH: Lapis lazuli

USAGE TIP: Malachite is believed to offer protection during air travel. Carry a small piece in a carry-on, handbag, or even your pocket when you fly.

MOLDAVITE

Moldavite is one form of a tektite (a class of rocks formed from a meteor impact), which makes it a "space rock." It is a high-vibration stone that is considered a synergy stone that works with 12 similar high-vibration stones (see below for specifics).

ORIGIN: Czech Republic, Germany, Moldova

LATTICE: Amorphous

SHAPES: Natural, chips

ENERGY: Amplifies

COLORS: Green

CHAKRA: Heart or crown

PLACEMENT: On or near the heart or crown chakra, as a necklace

HELPS WITH: Connecting to the Divine, calming anxiety and doubts, raising vibration, promoting meaningful dreams, rejuvenation

WORKS WITH: Azeztulite, brookite, danburite, herderite, natrolite, petalite, phenacite, satyaloka quartz, scolecite, tanzanite, tektite

USAGE TIP: Large pieces of moldavite can be costly but moldavite is a very powerful stone. Using even a small piece can have a profound effect.

MOONSTONE

Moonstone is a variety of feldspar characterized by milky color with an opalescent sheen called adularescence. Like other monoclinic stones, moonstone is a protective stone. It is also a stone that can connect you to higher realms, Divinity, and intuition.

ORIGIN: Austria, Brazil, India, Sri Lanka

LATTICE: Monoclinic

SHAPES: Natural, tumbled/polished, cut

ENERGY: Amplifies

COLORS: Black, peach, white

CHAKRA: Third eye or crown

PLACEMENT: On or near the third eye or crown chakra, as a necklace or earrings

HELPS WITH: Connecting to the Divine and strengthening intuition. Aiding in decision-making and rational thought, spurring creative problem-solving, facilitating self-expression, protection during water travel and nighttime travel

WORKS WITH: Rose quartz, amethyst

USAGE TIP: When spending time on the water or traveling at night, carry moonstone with you in a pocket or wear it as jewelry for protection.

OBSIDIAN

There are several varieties of obsidian, which is volcanic glass extruded as lava cools. Usually black in color (sometimes with spots, as in the case of snowflake obsidian), obsidian is a root chakra stone that can help protect and ground.

ORIGIN: All over the world

LATTICE: Amorphous

SHAPES: Natural, tumbled/polished, cut

ENERGY: Amplifies

COLORS: Black, black with white

CHAKRA: Root

PLACEMENT: On or near the root chakra, in the hands during grounding meditation

HELPS WITH: Aura cleansing, grounding, releasing anger and resentment, protection against negative energy

WORKS WITH: Clear quartz, selenite

USAGE TIP: If you're feeling foggy or energetically "congested," hold a piece of obsidian in your receiving (dominant) hand while breathing deeply.

ONYX

Onyx is a variety of chalcedony with parallel bands in the stone. It is a protective and grounding stone that can also aid in manifestation, and it can help balance excessive sexual desire.

ORIGIN: Brazil, Italy, Mexico, United States

LATTICE: Hexagonal

SHAPES: Natural, tumbled/polished, cut

ENERGY: Absorbs

COLORS: Black

CHAKRA: Root

PLACEMENT: On or near the root chakra, in pants pocket

HELPS WITH: Grounding, absorbing excessive sexual desire, improving harmony in intimate relationships, improving self-control, calming worry and tension, soothing nightmares

WORKS WITH: Agate, carnelian

USAGE TIP: Onyx on your bedside table or taped to a headboard can help balance intimate relationships.

OPAL

Prized for the luminescent play of light that flashes within them (called diffraction), opals are highly valued as a gemstone and a healing stone. However, because they lack a crystalline structure, opals aren't technically crystals. Opals are soft with a high water content, which makes them particularly delicate. Never cleanse an opal in water or salt.

ORIGIN: Australia, Canada, Great Britain, Mexico

LATTICE: Amorphous

SHAPES: Natural, tumbled/polished, cut

ENERGY: Amplifies

COLORS: Black, blue, colorless, green, orange, pink, red, violet, white, yellow

CHAKRA: Red or black—root orange—sacral, yellow—solar plexus, green or pink—heart, blue—throat, violet—third eye, colorless or white—crown

PLACEMENT: On or near any chakra, as jewelry of any type, near the head of your bed for dreaming

HELPS WITH: Creativity, inspiration, connection to the Divine and higher self, facilitating the flow of transformation, assisting in moving easily through obstacles, improving memory

WORKS WITH: Larimar

USAGE TIP: Store and use carefully, away from other crystals to prevent damage.

PERIDOT

Also known as olivine or chyrsolite, peridot has a beautiful green color that is prized as a gemstone. It is a stone of unconditional love, forgiveness, compassion, and other heart-focused emotions and experiences. It is also a cleansing and clearing stone.

ORIGIN: Egypt, Ireland, Russia, Sri Lanka

LATTICE: Orthorhombic

SHAPES: Natural, tumbled/polished, cut

ENERGY: Amplifies

COLORS: Green

CHAKRA: Heart

PLACEMENT: On or near your heart chakra, as a necklace or bracelet, as a ring on your commitment (ring) finger

HELPS WITH: Promoting positivity, all types of love, forgiveness, compassion, healing emotional trauma, lessening ego, prosperity, luck, aura cleansing, balancing chakras

WORKS WITH: Clear quartz, rose quartz, smoky quartz

USAGE TIP: Carry or wear peridot when you feel you need a little extra luck.

RHODOCHROSITE

Rhodochrosite is a vibrant, banded pink stone. When it is lighter pink, some people mistake it for rose quartz, and it has some similar metaphysical properties. In general, however, you can tell it's rhodochrosite instead of rose quartz by its deep, intense pink color and the white bands running through it.

ORIGIN: Argentina, Peru, Russia, Uruguay

LATTICE: Hexagonal

SHAPES: Natural, tumbled/polished, cut

ENERGY: Amplifies

COLORS: Pink

CHAKRA: Deep pink—root, light pink—heart

PLACEMENT: On or near your root or heart chakra, as a necklace or bracelet, as a ring on your commitment (ring) finger

HELPS WITH: Compassion, kindness, unconditional love, calming, grounding, forgiveness, aura cleansing, self-compassion

WORKS WITH: Rose quartz, clear quartz

USAGE TIP: If you're struggling with self-love or self-compassion, hold rhodochrosite in your receiving (nondominant) hand as you affirm, "I love myself unconditionally."

RUBY

Prized as a precious gemstone, ruby has a vibrant red color. Both rubies and sapphires are forms of corundum, a valued mineral. Along with finding ruby crystals by themselves, you may also find them embedded in fuchsite or zoisite. Ruby embedded in these stones is more affordable than ruby by itself and still has all the properties of a single ruby.

ORIGIN: India, Mexico, Russia

LATTICE: Hexagonal

SHAPES: Natural, tumbled/polished, cut

ENERGY: Amplifies

COLORS: Red

CHAKRA: Root and heart

PLACEMENT: On or near your root or heart chakra, as a necklace or bracelet, as a ring on your commitment (ring) finger

HELPS WITH: All types of love, opening the heart, expressing love, compassion, connection to spiritual and Divine love, trust, courage, forgiveness, grounding, clearing blocked emotions and energy

WORKS WITH: Sapphire, rose quartz

USAGE TIP: If you're stuck in any emotion, wear ruby jewelry or carry ruby in a pocket to help you break free of the blockage.

SAPPHIRE

Like rubies, sapphire is a form of the valued mineral corundum. While most people typically think of sapphires as blue, this gemstone comes in a variety of colors including orange, yellow, and pink. Sapphire is a stone of protection and manifestation.

ORIGIN: Australia, Brazil, Canada, India

LATTICE: Hexagonal

SHAPES: Natural, tumbled/polished, cut

ENERGY: Amplifies

COLORS: Blue, orange, pink, yellow

CHAKRA: Orange—sacral, yellow—solar plexus, blue—third eye or throat, pink—third eye

PLACEMENT: On or near the appropriate chakra, especially the throat chakra; as a necklace or earrings; near the head of your bed for insomnia

HELPS WITH: Self-expression, communication, sleep issues, speaking personal truth, loyalty, surrendering of personal will to Divine will

WORKS WITH: Ruby

USAGE TIP: Sapphire is particularly powerful when used with some type of vocal meditation, such as mantra meditations.

SELENITE

A variety of gypsum, selenite is a very soft crystal. Because of this, it's easy to carve and you'll often find it carved into interesting shapes and towers. It is primarily a protective stone. It is also a stone that doesn't need to be cleansed, as it doesn't absorb or store energy, and it serves as a cleansing stone for other crystals.

ORIGIN: China, France, India, United States

LATTICE: Monoclinic

SHAPES: Natural, tumbled/polished, carved, cut

ENERGY: Amplifies

COLORS: White

CHAKRA: Third eye and crown

PLACEMENT: On or near the third eye or crown chakra

HELPS WITH: Protecting against negativity, cleansing negative energy, cleansing other crystals, cleansing the aura, connection with intuition and the Divine, forgiveness

WORKS WITH: All stones

USAGE TIP: Due to selenite's softness, it can get damaged easily. Never expose it to water or salt, and store it separately from other crystals.

SODALITE

Sodalite is a natural amplifier that can help enhance energies you desire in your life. It can also help you balance energies if you have too much of one type and not enough of others.

ORIGIN: Australia, Brazil, Canada, Russia

LATTICE: Isometric

SHAPES: Natural, tumbled/polished, carved, cut

ENERGY: Amplifies

COLORS: Blue with white

CHAKRA: Throat and third eye

PLACEMENT: On or near the throat or third eye chakra, as a necklace or earrings

HELPS WITH: Speaking personal truth, communicating effectively, emotional balance, connection to intuition and spiritual guidance

WORKS WITH: Amethyst

USAGE TIP: Sodalite is an effective crystal if you are experiencing mood swings. Carry it with you or wear it as jewelry to help balance emotions.

TANZANITE

Tanzanite can help you release things that no longer serve you, and it can also help clear energetic blockages or clear away unwanted energy. The gemstone is named for where it was discovered—Tanzania.

ORIGIN: Tanzania

LATTICE: Orthorhombic

SHAPES: Natural, tumbled/polished, carved, cut

ENERGY: Amplifies

COLORS: Violet-blue

CHAKRA: Throat, third eye, and crown

PLACEMENT: On or near the throat, third eye, or crown chakra; as earrings or a necklace

HELPS WITH: Clearing away unwanted energy and things that don't serve you, promoting connection to higher self and connection to the Divine, integrating third eye and crown chakras, aiding in self-discovery and discovery of one's true spiritual nature

WORKS WITH: Clear quartz, celestite

USAGE TIP: Tanzanite can help you discover and clarify your own spiritual beliefs. Hold it in your receiving (nondominant) hand during meditation or prayer.

TIGERS EYE

Called so because of its resemblance to its namesake, tigers eye is most commonly known as a yellow/brown stone. However, there are also blue tigers eye and red tigers eye. It is a manifestation stone, and it can help you when struggling with issues of self.

ORIGIN: Brazil, Canada, India, South Africa

LATTICE: Hexagonal

SHAPES: Natural, tumbled/polished, carved, cut

ENERGY: Absorbs

COLORS: Blue, red, yellow

CHAKRA: Red—root, yellow—solar plexus, blue—throat

PLACEMENT: On or near the appropriate chakra, as a necklace or bracelet

HELPS WITH: Self-expression, self-worth, self-esteem, self-definition, self-love, self-concept, self-criticism, manifesting goals

WORKS WITH: Citrine

USAGE TIP: Avoid working with unpolished tigers eye, which contains asbestos. Polished tigers eye removes any threat from asbestos, but for safety, wash your hands after handling it.

TOPAZ

Topaz is a gemstone of exceptional clarity that can help you cleanse energies and release things that no longer serve you. It can also help align and balance energies. Golden topaz is the most commonly known form of the gem, but other colors occur as well, including blue, clear, pink, green, peach, and pink.

ORIGIN: Brazil, Canada, India, South Africa

LATTICE: Orthorhombic

SHAPES: Natural, clusters, tumbled/polished, carved, cut

ENERGY: Amplifies

COLORS: Blue, colorless, green, gold (most common), peach, pink, red, yellow

CHAKRA: Red—root, peach—sacral, yellow or gold—solar plexus, green—heart, blue—throat, pink—third eye, clear—crown

PLACEMENT: On or near the appropriate chakra, as any type of jewelry, around the perimeter or in the corners of any room that you want cleansed of negative energy

HELPS WITH: Self-expression, self-worth, self-esteem, self-definition, self-love, self-concept, self-criticism, manifesting goals, manifesting creative vision

WORKS WITH: Tanzanite, celestite

USAGE TIP: Hold or wear topaz when you state your affirmations or as you work on any creative projects.

TOURMALINE

While we discussed black tourmaline in the previous chapter as a stone of protection, other colors of tourmaline are also valuable healing stones. Tourmaline in any color can help you manifest qualities associated with the chakra color it matches. For example, green tourmaline can help you manifest unconditional love, while pink tourmaline can help you manifest romantic love.

ORIGIN: Afghanistan, Brazil, Sri Lanka, United States

LATTICE: Hexagonal

SHAPES: Natural, in quartz, tumbled/polished, carved, cut

ENERGY: Amplifies

COLORS: Black, green, green and pink (watermelon), orange, pink, red, yellow

CHAKRA: Red, black—root; orange—sacral; yellow—solar plexus; watermelon, pink, green—heart

PLACEMENT: On or near the appropriate chakra; as any type of jewelry, especially a bracelet or ring

HELPS WITH: Manifestation of desires, increasing vitality, rejuvenating and revitalizing, purification

WORKS WITH: Other tourmaline colors, selenite, aquamarine

USAGE TIP: Watermelon tourmaline, which is green and pink like watermelon, is a particularly powerful love manifestation stone. Use it during meditation in your giving (dominant) hand to help you love unconditionally.

ZIRCON

When I was a child and discovered that my birthstone was blue zircon, I felt totally ripped off because I thought it was the same thing as cubic zirconia, which is man-made. In fact, they're not related. Zircon is a naturally occurring mineral that protects and attracts.

ORIGIN: Australia, Canada, Pakistan, Sri Lanka

LATTICE: Tetragonal

SHAPES: Natural, tumbled/polished, carved, cut

ENERGY: Amplifies

COLORS: Blue, yellow

CHAKRA: Yellow—solar plexus, blue—throat or third eye

PLACEMENT: On or near the appropriate chakra; as any type of jewelry, especially a necklace or bracelet; at your desk at work for when you have tasks that underwhelm you

HELPS WITH: Self-love, spiritual growth, connection to the Divine, intuition, generating joy, increasing enthusiasm for things you may not be particularly excited about

WORKS WITH: Clear quartz, aquamarine

USAGE TIP: Naturally-occurring zircon is blue or yellow in color, but you may see the stone in other colors. If so, chances are that it has been heat-treated.

PART
3

Improve
Your Life
with
Crystals

CHAPTER

7

CRYSTAL PRESCRIPTIONS

In the pages that follow, I share crystal prescriptions I've discovered that work well with certain issues and conditions. Each issue listed offers a few different suggestions, as well as a mantra you can repeat before beginning your crystal work to interiorize and focus your mind. As mentioned throughout, choose the crystals that resonate with you the most.

Healing takes time. To spark change, you must be willing to allow it to enter your life. This requires an attitude of receptivity. As much as you can, try to set aside doubt or fear and enter a positive and receptive mind-set as you move into your healing sessions. Change only comes as you allow it and are willing to receive it. If you've never been one who receives well (and I find most people prefer to give), start your session with a positive statement such as, "I open myself to receive," or "I am grateful for that which I am about to receive."

ABUSE

Many people carry abuse as a burden that causes pain throughout their lives. Regardless of who has abused you, when they abused you, or the type of abuse (emotional, mental, physical, sexual), to truly live an empowered life you must work on releasing the pain you carry so you can move forward in strength.

MANTRA

I release myself from any harm I have sustained and move forward with self-compassion.

PRESCRIPTION #1—CARNELIAN

The results of abuse often settle in your sacral (or second) chakra, which is the center of personal power. This is especially true of physical and/or sexual abuse. Carnelian, which is orange, is therefore an effective second chakra stone.

Sitting or lying comfortably, hold a piece of carnelian in your receiving (nondominant) hand.

Close your eyes and visualize the pain from your abuse as a dark mass in your second chakra.

Visualize the dark mass exiting from where you are touching the ground (feet, bottom, back depending on whether you are sitting or lying) and draining into the Earth. The Earth will neutralize and rebalance the energy.

When you feel that the Earth has received all of the energy, hold the carnelian at your sacral chakra and repeat the mantra as many times as you wish. Take as long as you need, and do this as often as you need.

PRESCRIPTION #2—YELLOW TIGERS EYE

Self-worth and self-esteem often suffer as a result of abuse, particularly emotional and mental abuse. These are solar plexus chakra issues.

Hold a piece of yellow tigers eye in your receiving (nondominant) hand as you sit or lie quietly and comfortably. Close your eyes if that feels safe.

Visualize a golden light growing in your solar plexus, which is at the base of your sternum.

Repeat the mantra, and add an additional mantra for self-esteem such as, "I am worthy of good things." Do this for as long as you like.

PRESCRIPTION #3—ABUSE GRID

Create a crystal grid that helps with three issues that often arise from abuse: safety/security, personal power, and self-esteem. Here, we'll use a triangle grid that balances body, mind, and spirit. Place the grid underneath your bed or at your desk—or anywhere that you spend a lot of time. Cleanse the crystals about once a month. Any shape or size of stone will work. Make it pleasing to you.

CONFIGURATION: Triangle

FOCUS STONE: Black tourmaline (security, safety, absorbs negative energy)

INTENTION STONES: Citrine (self-esteem), rose quartz (self-love), carnelian (personal power)

PERIMETER STONES: Clear quartz (magnifies)

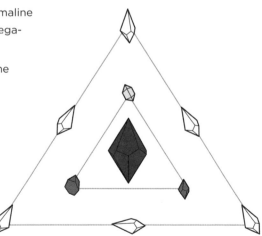

ADDICTION

While many people consider addiction to be strictly the purview of drugs and alcohol, addiction can be any seemingly unshakeable attachment that doesn't serve you, such as nonnutritious foods or an unhealthy relationship. These remedies will help strengthen personal will and release attachment as you work to free yourself from whatever your addiction may be.

MANTRA

I release all unhealthy attachments and move forward unencumbered.

PRESCRIPTION #1—HEMATITE

Addictions are primarily a root chakra issue, so using a crystal that helps balance the root chakra can be helpful. Since addiction is an issue of too much energy, you'll want a crystal that absorbs as opposed to one that amplifies, since you want to balance the chakra energy there. This makes hematite an excellent crystal for addiction.

Tape a small piece of hematite to the bottom of the place you sit most frequently, as well as to the bottom or the foot of your bed. You can also carry a piece of hematite in your pants pocket throughout the day or wear a hematite ring (replacing it if it breaks).

When you feel your addiction overcoming you, hold the hematite in your giving (dominant) hand, close your eyes, and repeat the mantra until the urge passes. Cleanse the hematite daily during this process.

PRESCRIPTION #2—AMETHYST

Amethyst is known as the "sobriety stone," as it was once believed to protect against drunkenness. If you are addicted to a mind-altering substance (including caffeine or nicotine), keep a piece of amethyst with you.

Hold the amethyst in your giving (dominant) hand, close your eyes, and say the mantra when you have an urge for the substance.

Repeat the mantra until the urge passes.

Cleanse the amethyst daily throughout this process.

PRESCRIPTION #3—CHAKRA LAYOUT

Create a simple layout of chakra stones somewhere you spend a lot of time, such as at your desk or in your bedroom. If in the bedroom, place the crystals under your bed with the black tourmaline below where your root chakra would be as you lie in bed and the howlite below where your crown chakra would be. These crystals absorb from each chakra the excessive energies associated with addiction.

CONFIGURATION: Vertical line

STONES (IN ORDER):
Howlite (crown chakra),
lapis lazuli (third eye chakra),
sodalite (throat chakra),
malachite (heart chakra),
yellow tigers eye (solar plexus chakra),
carnelian (sacral chakra),
black tourmaline (root chakra)

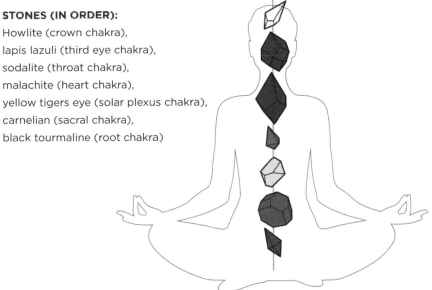

ANGER

We all get angry from time to time. I find the best way to deal with anger is to allow yourself to fully experience it because when you don't try to control it, it passes through you more quickly. However, if the anger gets stuck or if you have issues that result from excessive or long-term anger, such as rage, frustration, or resentment, then working with crystals can help you release and move forward.

MANTRA

I control my anger through calm and positive self-expression.

PRESCRIPTION #1—MALACHITE

Anger is often an issue of the heart chakra. It is an emotion of over-expression and excess energy, which means it needs to be absorbed and therefore requires an opaque crystal that can absorb the energy as you release it. The deep green of malachite balances heart chakra energy by absorbing excessive energy. After my husband's heart attack, I had him start wearing a long cord with a piece of malachite that hung at heart level, and that's my prescription here. Since rage and anger often settle into the heart and cause unbalanced and excessive energy, the malachite hanging at that level absorbs it effectively.

Hang a piece of malachite on a cord so the crystal hangs at heart level, and wear it throughout the day.

Cleanse the malachite daily.

If you feel anger rising and it won't pass, wrap your giving (dominant) hand around the malachite, close your eyes if that feels safe to you, and repeat the mantra.

PRESCRIPTION #2—RED OR BLACK JASPER

For anger that arises from fear (a common cause of anger because it serves as a defense mechanism when feeling afraid), you'll need an opaque black or red stone. Here, I recommend a piece of red or black jasper, carried in a pants pocket. When anger gets ahold of you and doesn't pass, ask yourself if it is a defense mechanism for fear.

Hold the jasper in your giving (dominant) hand and ground your feet firmly on the floor.

Visualize your anger as a dark red cloud draining through the bottom of your feet and into the Earth, which will neutralize it.

You can use the mantra here, as well.

PRESCRIPTION #3—ANGER RELEASE GRID

I recommend a simple circular grid. A circle stands for oneness and unity. The stones in this grid are designed to do two things: absorb the anger and amplify compassion. Place it anywhere you spend a lot of time or under your bed. Cleanse the stones, particularly the focus stone, every few days. Any shape or form of stone will work here.

CONFIGURATION: Circle

FOCUS STONE: Malachite (absorbs anger)

PERIMETER/INTENTION STONES: Rose quartz (amplifies compassion)

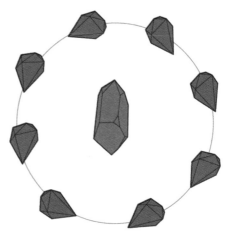

ANXIETY

Anxiety can be an occasional thing (worry), or it can be a chronic or even debilitating condition. There are multiple types of anxiety such as social anxiety, obsessive-compulsive disorders, phobias, and generalized anxiety. The prescriptions here are for persistent anxiety as opposed to short-term stress, which is covered in a separate prescription. Anxiety is another condition of excessive energy, so you need opaque stones that absorb, soothe, and calm.

MANTRA

I am peace.

PRESCRIPTION #1—AMBER

Amber can help support you when you are feeling anxious. For social anxiety, wear amber as a necklace, bracelet, or ring or carry a piece (carefully wrapped—it's delicate) in a pants pocket as you go into socially-intense situations. In such situations, the stone will help ease your anxiety.

Hold a piece of amber in your receiving (nondominant) hand and note the warmth of it.

Visualize a yellow light connecting from your solar plexus to the solar plexus of other people in the room.

Breathe deeply for as long as you need until the anxiety passes.

PRESCRIPTION #2—SODALITE

With its calming blue color, sodalite is the perfect anti-anxiety stone.

Hold a piece of sodalite in your giving (dominant) hand. Sit calmly. Close your eyes if that feels safe to you.

Visualize your anxiety flowing through you into your dominant arm, into your hand, and into the sodalite. As you visualize, repeat the mantra.

Do this at least once a day and cleanse the sodalite daily.

PRESCRIPTION #3
LAVENDER ESSENTIAL OIL AND AMETHYST

I used to have a lot of anxiety, and it would mostly come at night when I was trying to sleep. As a result, I spent a lot of sleepless nights with anxiety-induced insomnia. If you are like this and your anxiety always arises as you try to sleep, try this twofold remedy.

Fill your bathtub with warm water and add 4 drops of lavender essential oil. Soak for 10 to 20 minutes. As your anxieties arise, watch them drift away, and repeat the mantra or just the word "calm."

Sit in the tub as it drains and visualize your worries draining with the water. When the water is completely drained (and your anxieties with it), get out and dry off.

Then crawl into bed with a piece of amethyst taped underneath the head of your bed or on your bedside table (or both). Again, as anxieties arise, visualize them as clouds that drift harmlessly out of your head and into the universe. Repeat the mantra.

BALANCE

I find that when I am out of balance in any way, my life feels out of control and I feel unhappy until I am able to restore balance. Lack of balance manifests in many ways, such as poor work-life balance; excessive focus on body, mind, or spirit at the expense of the others; or too much stress without enough relaxation, just to name a few. The first step is recognizing you are out of balance in some way. Next, use these prescriptions as you seek to rebalance.

MANTRA

I am balanced in all things.

PRESCRIPTION #1—RAINBOW FLUORITE

Rainbow fluorite with its vast array of colors can help balance energies. Wear rainbow fluorite as jewelry when you feel out of balance.

A few times a day (such as when you wake up and when you go to bed), hold a piece of fluorite in your receiving (nondominant) hand.

Repeat the mantra.

PRESCRIPTION #2—TURQUOISE

Turquoise is a stone of harmony that can help balance your energies and bring you to a centered place of peace.

Wear turquoise jewelry as a great way to enjoy this stone as you seek balance.

Be sure to cleanse the turquoise every few days to retain its harmonic power.

PRESCRIPTION #3
BLACK TOURMALINE AND CLEAR QUARTZ

Black tourmaline and clear quartz work in harmony to create balanced energy throughout your system.

Lie on the floor or on a comfortable bed or sofa.

Place a piece of black tourmaline near your root chakra and a piece of quartz near your crown chakra. Close your eyes if that feels safe to you.

Visualize energy flowing from root to crown and back. Repeat the mantra if you wish.

BOUNDARIES

Setting healthy boundaries is something many people find difficult. However, maintaining these boundaries is essential for mental, spiritual, emotional, and physical health. Having firm boundaries in place protects your sense of self while still allowing you to interact with others in ways that are kind and compassionate, both to you and to another. However, boundaries can't be so firm that they don't allow for loving action when it is required. Therefore, they need to be firm but flexible and, ultimately, self-loving.

MANTRA

My boundaries are firm but flexible enough to allow for love.

PRESCRIPTION #1—YELLOW KYANITE

Yellow kyanite has two properties that make it a great stone for setting boundaries. First, it's part of the triclinic crystal system, which is a boundary or perimeter stone. Second, it supports the solar plexus chakra, which is where the energy of a healthy sense of self and boundaries resides.

As you meditate, hold a piece of yellow kyanite in your giving (dominant) hand and repeat the mantra.

Do this for 5 to 10 minutes, or until you feel your boundaries are firmly in place.

PRESCRIPTION #2—TURQUOISE

Turquoise, another triclinic crystal, is an excellent boundary setter. I recommend turquoise jewelry.

Put a piece of turquoise jewelry on in the morning.

Repeat the mantra as you visualize energy expanding from the turquoise and surrounding you.

PRESCRIPTION #3—LABRADORITE

Labradorite helps you find empowerment and connects you to your intuition, which helps you have the strength to set healthy boundaries. It is also a stone associated with the throat chakra, which can help you speak your truth, something necessary for giving voice to your boundaries.

When someone asks you to do something, take a moment and pause.

Hold a piece of labradorite in your hand and ask yourself, "Is this something that is within my personal boundaries to do?" See what answer arises.

It's okay to say no if you feel it is beyond your personal boundaries.

COMPASSION

Compassion, whether for self or others, is one of the most important qualities you can cultivate. Sometimes it's difficult to feel compassion, including self-compassion, but it is an essential high-vibration quality that allows us to experience ourselves, and others, as Divine.

MANTRA

Everything and everyone I see before me,
I see with the eyes of compassion.

PRESCRIPTION #1—ROSE QUARTZ

Compassion is an emotion that comes from your spirit and from your heart. Because the desire is to amplify compassion, using a stone that amplifies can help you grow and nurture this important quality. Rose quartz is one of the highest vibrational stones for cultivating compassion, and as a hexagonal system stone, it is also a natural amplifier.

For self-compassion, hold the rose quartz stone in your receiving (nondominant) hand and hold it at your heart.

For compassion for others, hold the rose quartz in your giving (dominant) hand and hold it at your heart.

Close your eyes if that feels safe to you. Repeat the mantra, feeling compassion moving through you.

PRESCRIPTION #2—AQUAMARINE

Sometimes it's difficult to experience compassion until you release judgment. Aquamarine is another hexagonal (amplifying) stone that can help you let go.

When you notice that judgment about yourself or another is blocking compassion, hold the aquamarine in your giving (dominant) hand and visualize releasing judgment.

As you hold the stone, repeat this mantra: "I release judgment. I allow compassion."

PRESCRIPTION #3—PERIDOT MEDITATION

Peridot is another stone of the heart, a stone of compassion.

Lie comfortably on your back and place a peridot on your heart chakra. Notice the beating of your heart. Close your eyes if that feels safe to you.

Visualize someone or something for whom you have tremendous compassion. Pull that feeling of love and compassion into your heart and feel it filling your body with every beat of your heart, moving through all your blood vessels into every part of your body and expanding beyond you and into the world.

Do this for as long as you like.

COURAGE

Courage isn't about not being afraid. It's about doing what you know to be the right thing for you, even when you are afraid. Courage is a trait that arises from the solar plexus chakra, so this is where we will focus the crystal prescriptions.

MANTRA

I have the courage to do what I know serves my highest and greatest good.

PRESCRIPTION #1—CITRINE

Citrine is a stone that amplifies, and its golden yellow color vibrates at the frequency of the solar plexus chakra. Therefore, it is a powerful stone of courage.

When you need courage, hold a piece of citrine in your receiving (nondominant) hand.

Repeat the mantra.

PRESCRIPTION #2—AQUAMARINE

Aquamarine is known as the stone of courage, so it's a wonderful stone to carry with you or wear as jewelry when you feel you need a boost of courage.

On days when you know you are going to have to do something outside of your comfort zone that will require courage, adorn yourself with an aquamarine bracelet, necklace, or ring.

Call on its energy to bring you courage. Repeat the mantra.

PRESCRIPTION #2—MALACHITE

With its opaque green color, malachite can absorb negative emotions like envy.

Lie on your back with the malachite on your heart. Close your eyes if that feels safe to you.

Visualize the envy flowing through you and into the malachite until you don't feel the envy any longer.

PRESCRIPTION #3—CARNELIAN AND APATITE

Carnelian helps you release envy, while apatite helps you focus on moving toward positive goals for yourself. This is a very powerful combination for releasing envy and jealousy because once you are making positive progress toward your own goals, you're less likely to focus on what others have that you don't. This is a simple meditation.

Sit or lie comfortably. Hold the carnelian in your receiving (nondominant) hand and the apatite in your giving (dominant) hand.

Visualize positive movement toward your goals flowing into you from the apatite and pushing the envy and jealousy out through your receiving hand and into the carnelian.

Cleanse the carnelian when you're done.

FORGIVENESS

Many people misunderstand forgiveness, believing it is about letting someone who has caused hurt off the hook. It isn't. Forgiveness is all about you choosing to no longer carry around pain you feel was caused by another's actions—or by your own actions. It is an act of self-love.

MANTRA

*I release the hurt of the past and
move forward in love.*

PRESCRIPTION #1—APACHE TEARS

Apache tears can help you overcome difficult and painful feelings, making them especially helpful when you need to release negative feelings so you can move forward and forgive.

Hold Apache tears in your giving (dominant) hand and visualize all your hurt feelings as a dark shadow flowing down your arm, down your hand, and into the crystal.

When you feel cleared, visualize the person you need to forgive and say, "I release you. I forgive you."

Repeat this as long as you like.

PRESCRIPTION #2—RHODOCHROSITE

Rhodochrosite is a lovely pink stone that can help with forgiveness.

Sit or lie comfortably and hold the rhodochrosite over your heart with both hands.

Repeat the mantra. Do this until you feel peace.

PRESCRIPTION #3
FORGIVENESS GRID AND MEDITATION

Create the grid for forgiveness on page 43 and place it near a spot where you can meditate comfortably. Sit or lie near the grid and visualize the person you wish to forgive. Imagine your energetic connection as ties extending between the two of you. Now visualize cutting the ties as you repeat the mantra, or say, "I release you." Once the ties are cut, visualize the person you need to forgive surrounded in white light.

GRATITUDE

Gratitude is such a powerful energetic state in which to exist. It is when you live in gratitude that real change occurs in your life, because it allows you to align with the truth of who you are. Gratitude focuses you on those things that truly matter.

MANTRA

I am grateful for all that I see, know, and experience.
I am grateful to be.

PRESCRIPTION #1—ROSE QUARTZ

Gratitude is a quality that arises from the heart chakra, so pink or green stones are especially powerful to help you manifest it. If you can find it, a heart-shaped rose quartz is a very powerful stone for gratitude—wear it as a pendant. If you don't have one that is heart shaped, any shape will do.

Wear a rose quartz crystal on a long cord so it hangs over your heart chakra.

PRESCRIPTION #2—AQUAMARINE

If expressing gratitude is difficult for you, a blue stone will activate your throat chakra, which can help with verbal expression. Aquamarine amplifies and helps manifest, so it can help you as you work to express your gratitude.

Wear aquamarine as a necklace.

Repeat the mantra a few times a day to help you express your gratitude more aptly.

PRESCRIPTION #3—GRATITUDE GRID

Create a heart-shaped grid in an area where you can meditate. Then sit near the grid. Close your eyes if that feels safe to you. Visualize gratitude flowing through your body and into your heart, and imagine your heart pumping gratitude throughout your entire body. Allow the gratitude to flow through and around you.

CONFIGURATION: Heart

FOCUS STONE: Rose quartz—heart shaped, if you've got it, otherwise any shape (self-love)

PERIMETER STONES: Clear quartz (magnifies)

GRIEF

Grief is the natural emotional result of loss, and it is necessary to allow yourself to experience it fully so it can pass through. However, if you become stuck in the grief, it is difficult to feel moments of joy and gratitude. Working with crystals can facilitate the grief passing through in a healthy way and help remove any blockages causing you to get stuck in the grief instead of moving forward.

MANTRA

I step into love to heal my pain.

PRESCRIPTION #1—APACHE TEARS

Apache tears are a well-known crystal remedy for grief. They won't make the grief go away, but they can help you process it in a healthy manner.

Sleep with Apache tears on your bedside table, and carry them with you as you process grief.

PRESCRIPTION #2—RUBY

Ruby is a stone that can help heal your heart when it is deeply wounded.

Sit or lie with the ruby held against your heart chakra.

Repeat the mantra as you visualize the healing light from the ruby entering you and filling you as it washes away your grief.

PRESCRIPTION #3—GRIEF GRID

Make a stages-of-grief grid and place it under your bed or near somewhere you spend a lot of time. Arrange the stones in a spiral with an
Apache tear as the first stone in the center and the following stones (in
order) spiraling outward: hematite (for anger), rainbow fluorite (for
denial), blue kyanite (for bargaining), smoky quartz (for depression),
and amethyst (for acceptance). Because of the unique configuration
of the stones, there isn't really a focus stone or perimeter stones here.
Instead, each stone helps you manage one stage of grief.

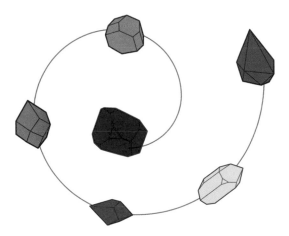

HAPPINESS

Happiness is a choice, but sometimes when we get bogged down in the stress and minutiae of our day-to-day lives, we forget that in order to cultivate happiness or joy, we only have to choose it. The crystal prescriptions that follow can help you remember to choose happiness regardless of the outward circumstances of your life.

MANTRA

I choose joy and happiness in every moment.

PRESCRIPTION #1—AMBER

For me, amber is the ultimate stone for happiness. It has a beautiful golden color and a natural warmth that radiates when you keep it next to your skin. Wearing amber jewelry can help you vibrate with the energy of happiness. It can also serve as a visual reminder to choose to be happy.

Hold the amber jewelry in your receiving (nondominant) hand. Repeat the mantra before putting it on.

PRESCRIPTION #2—SMOKY QUARTZ

Smoky quartz is a beautiful crystal for transmuting negative energy into positive energy. If you are going through a difficult or stressful period and find it difficult to be happy, meditate while holding a piece of smoky quartz in each hand.

Visualize your negative emotions flowing through your body and into your giving (dominant) hand and into the quartz you hold.

See the quartz changing the negative emotion to happiness.

Visualize the happiness flowing from the quartz in your giving (dominant) hand into the quartz in your receiving (nondominant) hand, up your arm and into your heart, which pumps it throughout your entire body.

PRESCRIPTION #3—CITRINE

Use citrine to help you be one who spreads happiness and joy.

Before you interact with others, hold a piece of citrine in your giving (dominant) hand and repeat this mantra: "Wherever I go and whomever I encounter, I spread happiness."

Place the crystal in a pocket and head out into the world. You can also charge small pieces of citrine in this manner and give them to people as gifts, to bring happiness to others.

INNER PEACE

All peace, whether it's personal peace, peace within relationships, peace within societies, or world peace, starts with inner peace. By being the calm regardless of what storm is raging outside, you set the vibrational example for others, and as others find peace through your example, they spread it as well. It is possible to be in this place of peace, even when the world seems at its darkest. And retreating to your peaceful place can help you weather even the most difficult times.

MANTRA

Regardless of what is happening around me,
I am at peace.

PRESCRIPTION #1—LARIMAR

Larimar, with its dreamy blue exterior, is a beautiful stone of peace and one of my current favorites (my favorites change with great frequency).

Use Larimar as a gazing stone.

Set it about a foot from your eyes and gaze at it as you repeat the mantra.

PRESCRIPTION #2—BLUE CALCITE

Blue calcite is another peaceful stone. It can help bring you peace even in the most stressful times, such as when adrenaline surges and you experience the fight-or-flight response.

Keep a piece of blue calcite with you and hold it in your receiving (nondominant) hand when you need peace.

Visualize the calm blue energy entering your hand through the crystal and flowing throughout your entire body.

PRESCRIPTION #3—PEACE GRID

The Serenity Prayer sets out a path to peace: changing what you can control, letting go of what you can't control, and understanding the difference. This crystal grid can help you achieve peace in even the most difficult of circumstances because it helps you let go, overcome the urge to control, and find inner peace and wisdom.

CONFIGURATION: Circle (oneness/unity)

FOCUS STONE: Turquoise (inner peace)

INTENTION STONES: Aquamarine (letting go)

PERIMETER STONES: Amethyst (wisdom)

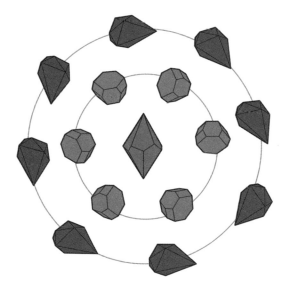

LOVE

When people ask me about crystals, the two most common requests for energetic assistance I receive are for prosperity and for love. While we all have love in our lives (even if we don't realize it) because we are unconditionally loved by the Divine, sometimes if we lack romantic love we feel lonely, and when we experience relationship difficulties, we fear we may lose love.

MANTRA

As I give love to others,
so do I receive love in gratitude.

PRESCRIPTION #1—ROSE QUARTZ

The most widely used crystal for romantic love (and all other kinds of love including unconditional love) is rose quartz. While it isn't strictly necessary, using a heart-shaped rose quartz is a nice touch.

If you are seeking romantic love or partnership, meditate with the rose quartz held against your heart chakra.

Visualize the energy of love coming out from your heart, passing through the crystal, and expanding into the universe in a way that is magnetic and will attract love. As you do, repeat the mantra.

PRESCRIPTION #2—PERIDOT

If you are experiencing difficulty within any relationship (romantic or otherwise), peridot is a good stone to help release anger and hurt feelings and bring loving, healing energy to the relationship.

Lie comfortably with a peridot on your heart chakra.

Visualize the person with whom you are experiencing difficulty. See a green light extending from your heart, through the peridot, and into the heart of the other person in the relationship you are trying to heal.

Repeat this mantra: "I allow love to heal the pain we have caused one another."

PRESCRIPTION #3—PINK TOURMALINE

If you are in a relationship where you feel there is a lack of trust and that is causing a block to love, try working with pink tourmaline, which can help build trust.

Hold the tourmaline in your giving (dominant) hand.

Visualize its energy surrounding both of you.

MOTIVATION

Accomplishing your dreams requires self-motivation. And I get it—sometimes you just feel a little less motivated than at other times. Motivation comes from the solar plexus chakra, which is a chakra of personal will. Imbalances of energy affect motivation, so rebalancing the energy with crystals can get you moving in a positive direction again.

MANTRA

As I choose, I do so I can be.

PRESCRIPTION #1—YELLOW TIGERS EYE

Yellow tigers eye is a stone that can amplify personal will.

Hold yellow tigers eye against your solar plexus chakra (or lie comfortably with it on your solar plexus) and repeat the mantra.

Alternatively, if you're trying to gather the motivation to do something specific, you can recite a mantra specific to that activity, such as, "I make food choices that support my overall health," for nutritious eating, or "I choose to live in a clean environment" to motivate you to clean up your space.

PRESCRIPTION #2—RAINBOW FLUORITE

Rainbow fluorite is an excellent stone to help you stay focused and motivated. A necklace or pendant is perfect for this use.

On days when you need some motivation, hold a rainbow fluorite necklace or pendant in your giving (dominant) hand.

Repeat the mantra before putting on the jewelry.

PRESCRIPTION #3—CITRINE AND ESSENTIAL OILS

Combine crystals with essential oils to help improve focus and motivation. Many essential oil companies make their own motivating blends (such as Young Living's Motivation or doTerra's Motivate), or you can use a single oil such as orange or lemon oil.

Diffuse the oil as you meditate, holding a citrine near your solar plexus chakra and repeating the mantra.

NEGATIVITY

Negativity can come from you or from other people or even world events, but however it comes it's an energy that bogs you down and makes it difficult to focus on creating positive things in your life. Plus, it's just not a lot of fun to be in a negative space. Working with crystals can help you transmute the negativity and focus on the positive.

MANTRA

I choose to be positive. Everything I see and experience, I see through a lens of the positive.

PRESCRIPTION #1—SMOKY QUARTZ

As I've previously mentioned, I have the perimeter of my entire property and my house surrounded with smoky quartz chips so that any energy that passes onto my property and into my personal space is converted into positive energy. You can certainly do this, but you don't need to take it that far.

Place smoky quartz under your bed or on your desk at work, and it will help convert the energy around you from negative to positive.

Cleanse the stone often, particularly if you are in a negative environment.

PRESCRIPTION #2—HEMATITE RING

Hematite is a stone that will absorb negativity whether it is coming from you, from others, or from the environment.

Wear a hematite ring or a ring with a black tourmaline stone.
Before putting the ring on, hold it in your hand and repeat the mantra.
Cleanse the stone regularly and replace the hematite ring if it breaks.

PRESCRIPTION #3—HIMALAYAN SALT LAMP

While I haven't listed it here in this book until now, pink Himalayan salt is a crystal, and it's a great way to create a positive environment in your space. Use a pink Himalayan salt lamp or candleholder (see the resources section on page 182) in a room where you spend a lot of time. When the warmth from the lightbulb or candle flame passes through the salt, it generates a positive energy field and cleanses negativity.

PATIENCE

Rumor around my household is that occasionally, under certain circumstances, I lack patience—which makes me pretty much like everyone else. Sometimes it's difficult to be patient, while other times we have the patience of saints. The following crystal prescriptions can help support you when you need a little extra.

MANTRA

This, too, shall pass. Everything is temporary.

PRESCRIPTION #1—HOWLITE

Howlite can help teach you patience. If you live a lifestyle where you often have to deal with impatience (young children, long lines at the bank, craziness in school parking lots), it's a good stone to use.

Keep a smooth piece of howlite in your pocket.

When you start to feel impatience rise, use the howlite as a worry stone and repeat the mantra.

PRESCRIPTION #2—AMAZONITE

If you suffer from generalized impatience (in other words, if you're just a generally impatient person), try amazonite, which can soothe jangled nerves and help you settle in and be more patient.

Keep a piece of amazonite in your pocket, or sleep with it next to or under your bed.

PRESCRIPTION #3—LABRADORITE

Sometimes what we truly need is patience with ourselves. Labradorite can help with this. I have labradorite all over my house and often wear it as jewelry, which may be why my patience has improved. I highly recommend labradorite jewelry.

Before you put a piece of labradorite jewelry on, hold it in your receiving (nondominant) hand.

Speak this mantra: "I am patient. I am at peace."

PROSPERITY

Many people struggle with prosperity, often because the belief in its opposite, lack, is so prevalent in our society. The key to establishing prosperity is believing there is enough and that you don't need to take something away from anyone else to be prosperous. While most people believe prosperity is about money, it is, in fact, about having an abundance of the things you value, including love, compassion, joy, friendship, health, and money.

MANTRA

I give thanks that I am prosperous.

PRESCRIPTION #1—CITRINE

Citrine is the most well-known prosperity stone. I like to combine citrine with feng shui (the Chinese system of arrangement of spaces to facilitate energy flow). Every room in your home has a prosperity corner, as does your entire house. To determine the prosperity corner for each room or the entire house, stand at the entrance to the room or house and look inward. The back left corner of each room and your house is the prosperity corner. If you're super great with directions or like to play with your compass, the southwest corner of each room and the house is also the wealth corner. Use one of these methods to determine the location of your prosperity corner.

Before you place the citrine, charge each piece by holding it in your giving (dominant) hand as you repeat the mantra.

Place citrine crystals in the prosperity corners of each room as well as the entire house.

PRESCRIPTION #2—AVENTURINE

Green aventurine is also a powerful attractor of prosperity.

Hold a piece of green aventurine in your receiving (nondominant) hand and visualize yourself as magnetic, drawing prosperity to you. Repeat the mantra for 5 to 10 minutes.

PRESCRIPTION #3—PROSPERITY GRID

Create a prosperity grid. Place it in your home's prosperity corner, as described in Prescription #1—Citrine on the previous page.

CONFIGURATION: *Vesica piscis* (creation)

FOCUS STONE: Citrine (prosperity)

INTENTION STONES: Turquoise (luck and prosperity)

PERIMETER STONES: Clear quartz (magnifies)

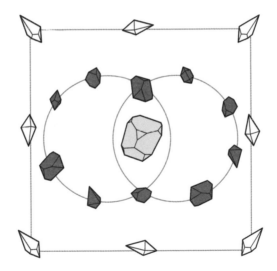

REGRET

Regret is an emotion that doesn't necessarily serve us well. I see regret as the long-term effects of unresolved guilt or shame, and when we have regrets, we fail to focus on those things we choose in life and instead focus on something we did or didn't choose. Regret keeps you focused on the past instead of remaining rooted in the here and now. Self-forgiveness is essential in overcoming regret.

MANTRA

I step away from my regrets of the past.
I forgive myself.

PRESCRIPTION #1—ROSE QUARTZ

Self-compassion lies at the root of releasing regret. Rose quartz is a beautiful crystal that can help you forgive yourself, step into a place of self-compassion, and release regret.

Lie on your back and place a rose quartz crystal on your heart. Close your eyes if that feels safe to you. Repeat the mantra.

PRESCRIPTION #2—SMOKY QUARTZ

Smoky quartz is a crystal that can help you release old beliefs, and what is regret if not an old belief system that no longer serves you?

Keep a piece of smoky quartz in your pocket.

If you feel regret overtaking you or find your mind slipping into the past, hold the smoky quartz in your giving (dominant) hand and repeat the mantra until your regret quiets.

Do this consistently.

PRESCRIPTION #3—RELEASING REGRET GRID

Make a grid for releasing regret. Place this grid under your bed or somewhere on a flat surface where you spend lots of time.

CONFIGURATION: Triangle (connects body, mind, spirit)

FOCUS STONE: Smoky quartz (releases old belief systems and transmutes negative to positive)

INTENTION STONES: Aquamarine (releases old patterns)

PERIMETER STONES: Black tourmaline (absorbs negativity)

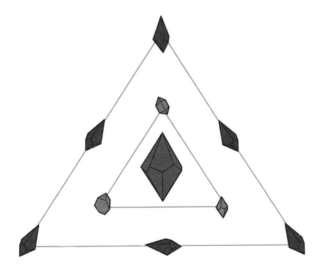

REJECTION

It hurts when you feel as if someone has rejected you, whether it's in a personal relationship or regarding something else, such as a job. Any time you put yourself "out there" in any way, you risk rejection. It's something that just happens in life, and you have no control over it. What you *can* control, however, is your reaction to rejection, or any fear of rejection that keeps you from trying new things.

MANTRA

Even when I am afraid, I take risks that serve my highest and greatest good.

PRESCRIPTION #1—ROSE QUARTZ

Rejection stings if we take it to heart. We have no control over whether somebody wants us, likes us, or chooses us, but that doesn't keep it from hurting when rejection happens. To heal the pain from rejection, you need to return to a place of self-love, and rose quartz is effective for this.

If you're hurting from the sting of rejection, wear rose quartz jewelry.

Visualize unconditional love flowing from the rose quartz throughout your entire body.

PRESCRIPTION #2—HEMATITE

Ultimately, overcoming a fear of rejection centers on overcoming fear. Fear is an emotion that starts in the root chakra and relates to safety and security.

Meditate with a hematite in your receiving (nondominant) hand.

As you repeat the mantra, visualize your fear of rejection as a black cloud flowing from your body and into the hematite.

Cleanse the stone after your meditation.

PRESCRIPTION #3—YELLOW TIGERS EYE

Rejection hits us right in the solar plexus, affecting our self-image and self-worth. Strengthening this chakra can help you overcome pain from past rejection and serve to immunize you against pain from rejection in the future, because if you have a strong sense of self-worth, you're less likely to suffer ill effects when you are rejected.

To use yellow tigers eye, lie comfortably on your back and place the crystal on your solar plexus chakra.

Visualize its energy flowing through you and strengthening your sense of self-worth.

SELF-CONFIDENCE

There's a fine line between self-confidence and arrogance. Some people may be overconfident without the skills or knowledge to back it up, while others may be highly capable but don't believe they deserve their accomplishments because they may be exposed as a "fraud." These are the two opposites of self-confidence: an overabundance and a lack of self-confidence. Right in the middle is the perfect balance that allows you to be successful, joyful, and confident, so it's essential to balance these energies.

MANTRA

I accept myself unconditionally.

PRESCRIPTION #1—YELLOW TIGERS EYE

Meditating with yellow tigers eye helps you build healthy self-confidence while absorbing any excesses that might cause you to move into arrogance.

Meditate while holding a piece of yellow tigers eye to your solar plexus chakra with your giving (dominant) hand.

Repeat this mantra: "I accept myself exactly as I am."

PRESCRIPTION #2—CITRINE

Citrine is a crystal that amplifies and also strengthens self-confidence.

Hold citrine in your receiving (nondominant) hand as you meditate while speaking the mantra.

Visualize the golden light from the citrine surrounding you completely and flowing through you as self-confidence.

PRESCRIPTION #3—AMBER

Amber supports solar plexus chakra energies and projects its own confident warmth.

I recommend wearing amber jewelry if you fall on either end of the spectrum of self-confidence. A necklace or bracelet is the perfect location for the amber.

STRESS

Modern life is stressful. Not only do we have the daily stressors of our life, such as jobs, family obligations, and personal activities, but we also experience the stress of world events and concerns that often seem to be spiraling out of control. However, managing stress is essential for overall good health and balance.

MANTRA

Release.

PRESCRIPTION #1—YELLOW TIGERS EYE

Stress affects your adrenal glands, which are associated with your solar plexus chakra. Yellow tigers eye can absorb excess energy that can cause imbalance as the result of stress and help you rebalance.

Lie on your back with a yellow tigers eye on your solar plexus chakra.

Breathe deeply and repeat the mantra as many times as you need until you feel calm.

PRESCRIPTION #2—SMOKY QUARTZ

Smoky quartz has a very stabilizing energy that can help you quickly regain balance when you go into fight-or-flight mode due to a stressful situation. This is one stone I carry with me pretty much all the time because I find it so soothing and balancing when I feel stressed.

When you notice stress, hold the smoky quartz in either hand.

Close your eyes if that feels safe to you. Breathe in. As you breathe out, repeat the mantra.

Do this for as long as it takes to calm your stress.

PRESCRIPTION #3—HEMATITE

Stress is essentially a fear reaction, and hematite is one of the best stones for absorbing fear.

Hold the hematite in your receiving (nondominant) hand when you experience stress.

See the stress energy as a black cloud flowing from you and into the hematite.

Cleanse the hematite after each use for stress.

TRUST

Trust comes only if you believe you will be safe and secure. Many people who experienced emotional, physical, or mental traumas in childhood (even mild traumas, which pretty much means all of us) occasionally struggle with trust because at some point they've interpreted an experience as meaning they are not safe. Therefore, the way to establish trust is to work on all the ways you notice you are safe and secure.

MANTRA

I trust in the benevolence of the universe.
I am safe.

PRESCRIPTION #1—GARNET

Safety and security issues settle in the root chakra, so balancing this chakra's energies are essential for feeling safe enough to trust.

Sit or lie comfortably and place the garnet near your root chakra.
Close your eyes if that feels safe to you.
Breathe deeply and repeat the mantra.

PRESCRIPTION #2—CARNELIAN

What if it's yourself you feel you can't trust? Many of us are far more likely to break the promises we make to ourselves than those we make to others, which can lead to a lack of trust in self. Lack of integrity (including with self) is a sacral chakra issue, and carnelian can balance this chakra.

Lie comfortably and place the carnelian on your sacral chakra.
Repeat this mantra: "I trust myself because I keep my word to myself."

PRESCRIPTION #3—AMETHYST

Another thing people often feel they can't trust is the universe in general. They may feel life is generally unsafe and act from this. Amethyst helps connect you to Divine guidance, and following Divine guidance to good results leads to greater trust in the universe.

Place the amethyst on your third eye chakra.
Meditate as you repeat the mantra.

Identify Your Crystal
A Color Guide

	BLACK		
	APACHE TEARS		BLACK CALCITE
	HEMATITE		BLACK JADE
	BLACK JASPER		BLACK KYANITE
	LODESTONE		OBSIDIAN
	ONYX		BLACK OPAL
	BLACK TOURMALINE		

BLUE

	BLUE LACE AGATE		BLUE APATITE
	AQUAMARINE		BLUE AVENTURINE
	BLUE CALCITE		BLUE CHALCEDONY
	BLUE FLUORITE		BLUE KYANITE
	LABRADORITE		LAPIS LAZULI
	LARIMAR		SAPPHIRE
	SODALITE		TANZANITE
	BLUE TIGERS EYE		TURQUOISE

BROWN

	BROWN AGATE		BROWN APATITE
	ORANGE AVENTURINE		JASPER

GRAY

	BLACK OR GRAY AGATE		BOTSWANA AGATE
	GRAY AVENTURINE		SMOKY QUARTZ

GREEN

	MOSS AGATE		AMAZONITE
	GREEN AVENTURINE		GREEN CALCITE
	EMERALD		EPIDOTE
	GREEN FLUORITE		FUCHSITE
	TSAVORITE GARNET		GREEN JADE
	MALACHITE		MOLDAVITE
	PERIDOT		GREEN TOURMALINE

ORANGE/PEACH

	ORANGE APATITE		ORANGE AVENTURINE
	CARNELIAN		HESSONITE GARNET
	PEACH MOONSTONE		FIRE OPAL
	PADPARADSCHA SAPPHIRE		

MULTICOLORED

	BANDED AGATE		AMETRINE
	RAINBOW FLUORITE		WATERMELON TOURMALINE

PINK

	PINK APATITE		PINK CALCITE
	PINK DANBURITE		PINK FLUORITE
	RHODOCHROSITE		ROSE QUARTZ
	PINK TOURMALINE		

PURPLE

	PURPLE AGATE		AMETHYST
	PURPLE CALCITE		PURPLE FLUORITE
	LAVENDER JADE		

RED			
	RED AGATE		RED CALCITE
	RED GARNET		RED JADE
	RED JASPER		RUBY
	RED TIGERS EYE		

WHITE/CLEAR

	WHITE AGATE		WHITE CALCITE
	DANBURITE		COLORLESS FLUORITE
	HOWLITE		WHITE JADE
	MOONSTONE		OPAL
	CLEAR QUARTZ		SELENITE

YELLOW/GOLD

	YELLOW AGATE		AMBER
	YELLOW APATITE		YELLOW AVENTURINE
	YELLOW CALCITE		CITRINE
	YELLOW DANBURITE		YELLOW FLUORITE
	YELLOW JADE		YELLOW KYANITE
	YELLOW TIGERS EYE		TOPAZ

Glossary

AFFIRMATION A statement of positive intent

AGGREGATE A substance that is a combination of several minerals without a crystalline structure

AURA An energy field extending out beyond the body

CHAKRA Energy centers that connect the physical to the nonphysical

CHARGING A method of adding intention to a crystal's energy

CLEANSING Clearing energy from crystals so they can resonate at their own frequency

CRYSTAL SYSTEM The various systems into which crystals are categorized based on the crystalline lattice patterns

DIVINE Higher realms

ENERGY The substance that underlies all matter in the universe

ENTRAINMENT Two energetic systems with different vibrations synchronizing when placed near each other

GIVING HAND The hand that sends energy out from your body, typically your dominant hand

GROUNDING Rooting your energy to the energy of the Earth

HEXAGONAL One form of crystal system structure; hexagonal crystals are manifestors energetically

HIGHER CONSCIOUSNESS Your higher self, the part of you that is Divine, your soul

INTUITION Information coming from higher consciousness

ISOMETRIC One form of crystal system structure; energetically isometric crystals are amplifiers

MANTRA Anything you chant during meditation to focus your mind

MONOCLINIC One form of crystal system structure; energetically monoclinic stones are protectors

ORTHORHOMBIC One form of crystal system structure; energetically orthorhombic crystals are cleansers, clearers, and releasers

RECEIVING HAND The hand through which you receive energy, typically your nondominant hand

TETRAGONAL One form of crystal system structure; energetically hexagonal crystals help you achieve your desires

TRICLINIC One form of crystal system structure; energetically triclinic crystals set boundaries and ward off energies

WORRY STONE A smooth, flat stone you rub your thumb over

Resources

WEBSITES

Amazon.com Offers a nice selection of Himalayan salt lamps. Enter "Himalayan salt lamp" in the search field.

Crystal-Cure.com Crystal products and information about crystals and their properties.

HealingCrystals.com My favorite crystal shop online with lots of great information about crystals, as well as plenty of crystals for shopping.

Minerals.net A database with scientific and technical information about minerals.

Myss.com The website of author Caroline Myss, who offers great information about chakras.

BOOKS

The Chakra Bible: The Definitive Guide to Working with Chakras by Patricia Mercier (New York: Sterling Publishing, 2007)

Crystals for Healing: The Complete Reference Guide with Over 200 Remedies for Mind, Heart & Soul by Karen Frazier (Berkeley, CA: Althea Press, 2015)

Higher Vibes Toolbox: Vibrational Healing for an Empowered Life by Karen Frazier (La Vergne, TN: Afterlife Publishing, 2017)

The Subtle Body: An Encyclopedia of Your Energetic Anatomy by Cyndi Dale (Louisville, CO: Sounds True, 2014)

APPS

Bowls—Authentic Tibetan Singing Bowls (Oceanhouse Media, 2015)

Crystal Guide Pocket Edition by Mark Stevens (Mark Stevens, 2017)

New Age Stones and Crystal Guide by August Hesse (Star 7 Engineering, 2010)

Solfeggio Sonic Sound Healing Meditations by Glenn Harrold and Ali Calderwood (Diviniti Publishing, 2017)

References

Crystal Age. "A Brief History of Crystals and Healing." Accessed June 13, 2017. www.crystalage.com/crystal_information/crystal_history/.

———. "The Seven Crystal Systems." Accessed June 13, 2017. www.crystalage.com/crystal_information/seven_crystal_systems/.

Dictionary.com. "Piezoelectric Effect." Accessed June 13, 2017. www.dictionary.com/browse/piezoelectric-effect.

GemSelect. "How Gemstones Get Their Colors." March 11, 2008. Accessed June 13, 2017. www.gemselect.com/other-info/about -gemstone-color.php.

Golombek, D. A., and R. E. Rosenstein. "Physiology of Circadian Entrainment." *Physiological Reviews* 90, no. 3 (July 2010): 1063–102. doi:10.1152/physrev.00009.2009.

Hadni, A. "Applications of the Pyroelectric Effect." *Journal of Physics E: Scientific Instruments* 14, no. 11 (November 1981): 1233–240. iopscience .iop.org/article/10.1088/0022-3735/14/11/002/pdf.

Larson Jewelers. "What Is the Difference Between a Gemstone, Rock, and Mineral?" May 17, 2016. Accessed June 13, 2017. blog.larsonjewelers .com/difference-between-a-gemstone-rock-and-mineral/.

Minerals Education Coalition. "Quartz." Accessed June 13, 2017. mineralseducationcoalition.org/minerals-database/quartz/.

Online Dictionary of Crystallography. "Crystal System." June 7, 2017. Accessed June 13, 2017. reference.iucr.org/dictionary/Crystal_system.

ScienceDaily. "Pyroelectricity." Accessed June 13, 2017. www.sciencedaily.com/terms/pyroelectricity.htm.

Shea, Neil. "Cavern of Crystal Giants." *National Geographic.* November 2008. Accessed June 13, 2017. http://ngm.nationalgeographic.com/2008/11/crystal-giants/shea-text.

Starr, Michelle. "Quartz Crystal Computer Rocks." CNET. May 19, 2014. Accessed June 13, 2017. www.cnet.com/news/quartz-crystal-computer-rocks/.

Thompson, R. J., Jr. "The Development of the Quartz Crystal Oscillator Industry of World War II." *IEEE Trans Ultrason Ferroelectr Freq Control* 52, no. 5 (May 2005): 694–7. www.ncbi.nlm.nih.gov/pubmed/16048172.

The Watch Company, Inc. "Quartz Watches." WatchCo.com. Accessed June 13, 2017. www.watchco.com/quartz-watches/.

Index

A

Absorbers. *See* Energy absorbers

Abuse prescriptions, 120–121

Addiction prescriptions, 122–123

Affirmative meditation, 48

Agate, 76

Amazonite

  about, 77

  courage grid, 135

  patience prescription, 157

Amber

  about, 8, 78

  anxiety prescription, 126

  happiness prescription, 146

  self-confidence prescription, 165

Amethyst. *See also* Citrine

  about, 20, 54–55

  addiction prescription, 123

  anxiety prescription, 127

  creativity grid, 43

  decisiveness prescription, 136

  grief grid, 145

  pairing, 27

  peace grid, 149

  third eye grid, 137

  trust prescription, 169

Ametrine

  about, 79

  decisiveness prescription, 137

Amorphous crystals

  about, 6, 26

  amber, 78

  Apache tears, 80

  moldavite, 100

  obsidian, 102

  opal, 104

Amplifiers. *See* Energy amplifiers

Anger prescriptions, 124–125

Anxiety prescriptions, 126–127

Apache tears

  about, 80

  forgiveness prescription, 140

  grief grid, 145

  grief prescription, 144

  pairing, 27

Apatite

  about, 81

  envy prescription, 139

Aquamarine

  about, 82

  compassion prescription, 133

  courage grid, 135

  courage prescription, 134

  gratitude prescription, 142

  peace grid, 149

  releasing regret grid, 161

Aventurine
about, 83
envy prescription, 138
prosperity prescription, 159

B
Balance prescriptions, 128–129
Beryls, 87
Black tourmaline
about, 20, 56–57
abuse grid, 121
balance prescription, 128
pairing, 27
releasing regret grid, 161
Blades, 22
Body, 32
Boundary-setting
prescriptions, 130–131

C
Calcite
about, 84
inner peace prescription, 148
Carnelian
about, 20, 58–59
abuse grid, 121
abuse prescription, 120
envy prescription, 139
trust prescription, 169

Chakras, 44–45, 49, 123. *See*
also specific crystals
Chalcedony, 85. *See also* Onyx
Chyrsolite. *See* Peridot
Circadian rhythm, 9
Circles, 42
Citrine
about, 20, 60–61
abuse grid, 121
courage grid, 135
courage prescription, 134
creativity grid, 43
happiness prescription, 147
motivation prescription, 153
pairing, 27
prosperity grid, 159
prosperity prescription, 158
self-confidence prescription, 165
Cleansing, 33, 49
Clear quartz
about, 20, 62–63
abuse grid, 121
balance prescription, 128
courage grid, 135
forgiveness grid, 43, 141
gratitude grid, 143
pairing, 27
prosperity grid, 159
third eye grid, 137

Clusters, 22
Color
    chakras, 44–47
    crystals, 6, 171–179
Compassion prescriptions, 132–133
Courage prescriptions, 134–135
Crown (seventh) chakra, 45, 49
Crystal grids
    about, 42–43
    abuse, 121
    anger release, 125
    courage, 135
    creativity, 43
    forgiveness, 43, 141
    gratitude, 143
Crystal grids (continued)
    grief, 145
    peace, 149
    prosperity, 159
    releasing regret, 161
    third eye, 137
Crystals. See also specific crystals;
        specific prescriptions
    about, 6, 8
    brand names, 23–24
    buying, 19
    choosing, 24–26, 35
    cleansing, 33, 49
    and color, 6, 171–179
    energy of, 9–10, 12–13, 31
    and healing, 5, 32, 35–36
    and individual needs, 14
    lattice patterns, 6–7
    maintaining, 34

myths about, 13, 15
natural vs. lab-made, 8–9
pairing, 26–27
programming, 34
safety, 38–39
shapes, 22–23, 25
shopping tips, 28–29
storing, 38
in technology, 11
workhorse, 20–21, 54–73
Crystal systems, 6–7, 24, 26
Cueva de los Cristales (Cave
        of Crystals), 28
Cut stones, 23

D

Danburite, 86
Decisiveness prescriptions, 136–137
Diamonds, 8
Dodecahedrons, 25

E

Electricity, 9–10
Elixirs, 35
Emerald, 87
Energy, 9–10, 12–13, 31
Energy absorbers
    amazonite, 77
    amber, 78
    Apache tears, 80
    black tourmaline, 56–57
    carnelian, 58–59
    fluorite, 64–65
    fuchsite, 89

hematite, 66–67

howlite, 91

jade, 92

jasper, 93

lapis lazuli, 96

Larimar, 97

malachite, 99

onyx, 103

tigers eye, 112

turquoise, 72–73

Energy amplifiers

agate, 76

amber, 78

amethyst, 54–55

ametrine, 79

apatite, 81

aquamarine, 82

aventurine, 83

calcite, 84

chalcedony, 85

citrine, 60–61

clear quartz, 62–63

danburite, 86

emerald, 87

epidote, 88

garnet, 90

labradorite, 95

lodestone, 98

moldavite, 100

moonstone, 101

obsidian, 102

opal, 104

peridot, 105

rhodochrosite, 106

rose quartz, 68–69

ruby, 107

sapphire, 108

selenite, 109

smoky quartz, 70–71

sodalite, 110

tanzanite, 111

topaz, 113

tourmaline, 114

zircon, 115

Entrainment, 9–10, 33

Envy prescriptions, 138–139

Epidote, 88

Essential oils

anxiety prescription, 127

motivation prescription, 153

F

Fluorite, 64–65. *See also*
       Rainbow fluorite

Forgiveness prescriptions, 140–141

Fuchsite, 89

G

Garnet

about, 90

pairing, 27

trust prescription, 168

Gems, 8

Geodes, 22

Gratitude prescriptions, 142–143

Grids. *See* Crystal grids

Grief prescriptions, 144–145

H

Happiness prescriptions, 146–147

Healing. *See also specific prescriptions*

body, mind, and spirit, 32

choosing a crystal for, 35

and intention, 34, 37

sound, 49

tips for, 35–36

Heart (fourth) chakra, 44–45, 49

Hematite

about, 20, 66–67

addiction prescription, 122

grief grid, 145

negativity prescription, 155

rejection prescription, 162

stress prescription, 167

Hexagonal crystals

about, 7, 24

agate, 76

amethyst, 54–55

ametrine, 79

apatite, 81

aquamarine, 82

aventurine, 83

black tourmaline, 56–57

calcite, 84

carnelian, 58–59

chalcedony, 85

citrine, 60–61

clear quartz, 62–63

emerald, 87

hematite, 66–67

jasper, 93

onyx, 103

rhodochrosite, 106

rose quartz, 68–69

ruby, 107

sapphire, 108

smoky quartz, 70–71

tigers eye, 112

tourmaline, 114

Hexahedrons, 25

Himalayan salt, 155

Howlite

about, 91

patience prescription, 156

I

Icosahedrons, 25

Inner peace prescriptions, 148–149

Intention, 34, 37

Isometric crystals

about, 7, 24

fluorite, 64–65

garnet, 90

sodalite, 110

J

Jade, 92

Jasper

about, 93

anger prescription, 125

Jealousy. *See* Envy prescriptions

K

Kyanite

about, 94

boundary-setting prescription, 130

grief grid, 145

L

Labradorite
  about, 95
  boundary-setting prescription, 131
  pairing, 27
  patience prescription, 157
Lapis lazuli, 96
Larimar
  about, 97
  inner peace prescription, 148
Lattice patterns, 6–7, 24, 26
Lodestone, 98
Love prescriptions, 150–151

M

Magnetite. *See* Lodestone
Maintenance, 34
Malachite
  about, 99
  anger prescription, 124
  anger release grid, 125
  envy prescription, 139
Mantras, 48. *See also specific*
  prescriptions
Marble, 8
Meditation, 48
Merkabas, 25
Mind, 32
Minerals, 8
Moldavite, 100
Monoclinic crystals
  about, 7, 24
  amazonite, 77
  chalcedony, 85

epidote, 88
  fuchsite, 89
  howlite, 91
  jade, 92
  lodestone, 98
  malachite, 99
  moonstone, 101
  selenite, 109
Moonstone, 101
Motivation prescriptions, 152–153
Muscle testing, 35

N

Natural stones, 22–23
Negativity prescriptions, 154–155

O

Obsidian, 102. *See also* Apache tears
Octahedrons, 25
Olivine. *See* Peridot
Onyx, 103
Opal, 8, 104
Orthorhombic crystals
  about, 7, 24
  danburite, 86
  peridot, 105
  tanzanite, 111
  topaz, 113
Oscillators, 11

P

Patience prescriptions, 156–157
Pearls, 8
Pectolite. *See* Larimar

Peridot
   about, 105
   compassion prescription, 133
   love prescription, 151
Phenacite, 14
Piezoelectric effect, 10
Points, 22
Polished stones, 23
Programming, 34
Prosperity prescriptions, 158–159
Pyroelectric effect, 10

Q

Quartz. *See also* Chalcedony;
   Clear quartz; Rose
   quartz; Smoky quartz
   about, 15
   cleansing with, 33
   in technology, 11

R

Rainbow fluorite
   about, 20
   balance prescription, 128
   grief grid, 145
   motivation prescription, 153
Regret prescriptions, 160–161
Rejection prescriptions, 162–163
Rhodochrosite
   about, 106
   forgiveness prescription, 141
Rocks, 8
Root (first) chakra, 44–45, 49
Rose quartz

about, 20, 68–69
abuse grid, 121
anger release grid, 125
compassion prescription, 132
gratitude grid, 143
gratitude prescription, 142
love prescription, 150
pairing, 27
regret prescription, 160
rejection prescription, 162
Rough crystals, 22
Rough/raw stones, 22–23
Ruby
   about, 107
   grief prescription, 144
   pairing, 27

S

Sacral (second) chakra, 44–45, 49
Sacred geometry, 25, 42–43
Safety, 38–39
Sage, 33
Sapphire, 108
Schorl. *See* Black tourmaline
Selenite
   about, 109
   forgiveness grid, 43, 141
Self-confidence
   prescriptions, 164–165
Singing bowls, 49
Smoky quartz
   about, 20, 70–71
   grief grid, 145
   happiness prescription, 147

negativity prescription, 154
pairing, 27
regret prescription, 160
releasing regret grid, 161
stress prescription, 167
Sodalite
about, 110
anxiety prescription, 127
Solar plexus (third) chakra, 44–45, 49
Sound vibration, 49
"Space rocks." *See* Moldavite
Spheres, 25
Spirals, 42
Spirit, 32
Squares, 42
Stress prescriptions, 166–167

T
Tanzanite, 111
Tektite, 100
Tetragonal crystals
about, 7, 24
zircon, 115
Tetrahedron, 25
Third eye (sixth) chakra, 45, 49
Throat (fifth) chakra, 44–45, 49
Tigers eye, 112. *See also*
    Yellow tigers eye
Topaz, 113
Tourmaline. *See also* Black tourmaline
about, 114
love prescription, 151
Triangles, 42
Triclinic crystals

about, 7, 26
kyanite, 94
labradorite, 95
Larimar, 97
turquoise, 72–73
Trust prescriptions, 168–169
Turquoise
about, 20, 72–73
balance prescription, 128
boundary-setting prescription, 131
peace grid, 149
prosperity grid, 159

V
Vesica piscis, 42
Vibration
and entrainment, 9–10
sound, 49

W
Wands, 23
Worry. *See* Anxiety prescriptions

Y
Yellow tigers eye
abuse prescription, 121
motivation prescription, 152
rejection prescription, 163
self-confidence prescription, 164
stress prescription, 166

Z
Zircon, 115

Additional Credits

Page 21: Albert Russ/Shutterstock.com (hematite); Hapelena/Shutterstock.com (smoky quartz); J. Palys/Shutterstock.com (rose quartz, clear quartz, yellow citrine, rainbow fluorite & black tourmaline); Sergey Lavrentev/Shutterstock.com (amethyst); Verbaska/Shutterstock.com (turquoise); Mivr/Shutterstock.com (carnelian); page 27: Ozef/Shutterstock.com (labradorite); Vvoe/Shutterstock.com (apache tears); Albert Russ/Shutterstock.com (ruby); page 76: Verbaska/Shutterstock.com (rough); Afitz/Shutterstock.com (polished); page 77: Marcel Clemens/Shutterstock.com (rough); Phodo/iStock (polished); page 78: Humbak/Shutterstock.com (rough); Bestfotostudio/iStock (polished); page 79: PNSJ88/Shutterstock.com (rough); VvoeVale/iStock (polished); page 80: Shutterstock.com (rough); page 81: Imfoto/Shutterstock.com (rough); VvoeVale/iStock (polished); page 82: J. Palys/Shutterstock.com (rough); VvoeVale/iStock (polished); page 83: J. Palys/Shutterstock.com (rough); Verbaska/Shutterstock.com (polished); page 84: Ratchanat Bua-Ngern/Shutterstock.com (rough); Photo/iStock (polished); page 85: VvoeVale/iStock (rough); Reload Studio/iStock (polished); page 87: Imfoto/Shutterstock.com (rough); Byjeng/Shutterstock.com (cut); page 88: Vvoe/Shutterstock.com; page 89: Marcel Clemens/Shutterstock.com (rough); Vvoe/Shutterstock.com (polished); page 90: Rep0rter/iStock (rough); Vvoe/Shutterstock.com (polished); page 91: Miriam Doerr Martin Frommherz/Shutterstock.com (rough); Verbaska/Shutterstock.com (polished); page 92: Kongsky/Shutterstock.com (rough); SirChopin/Shutterstock.com (polished); page 93: DrPas/iStock (rough); Verbaska/Shutterstock.com (polished); page 94: Stefan Malloch/iStock (rough); Vvoe/Shutterstock.com (polished); page 95: J. Palys/Shutterstock.com (rough); page 96: J. Palys/Shutterstock.com (rough); Oliver Mohr/Shutterstock.com (polished); page 97: Kakabadze George/Shutterstock.com (rough); Oleg1/iStock (polished); page 98: Vitaly Raduntsev/Shutterstock.com (rough); page 99: Mali Lucky/Shutterstock.com (rough); Madien/Shutterstock.com (polished); page 100: Stellar Gems/Shutterstock.com (rough); page 101: Vvoe/Shutterstock.com (rough); page 102: Only Fabrizio/Shutterstock.com (rough); PNSJ88/Shutterstock.com (polished); page 103: J. Palys/Shutterstock.com (rough); Nastya Pirieva/Shutterstock.com (polished); page 104: Michael C. Gray/Shutterstock.com (rough); Alexander Hoffmann (polished); page 105: Albert Russ/Shutterstock.com (rough); Vvoe/Shutterstock.com (polished); page 106: PNSJ88/Shutterstock.com (rough); Vvoe/Shutterstock.com (polished); page 107: Bigjo5/iStock (polished); page 108: Imfoto/Shutterstock.com (rough); TinaImages/Shutterstock.com (polished); page 109: VvoeVale/iStock (rough); Only Fabrizio/Shutterstock.com (polished); page 110: Optimarc/Shutterstock.com (rough); VvoeVale/iStock (polished); page 111: PNSJ88/Shutterstock.com (rough); page 112: J. Palys/Shutterstock.com (rough); Coldmoon Photoproject/Shutterstock.com (polished);

PRESCRIPTION #3—COURAGE GRID

Amazonite is another stone of courage. Create a courage grid using aquamarine and citrine above and below with amazonite as the focus or center stone and quartz points as perimeter stones to direct and amplify the energy. Place it anywhere you spend a lot of time.

CONFIGURATION: Square

FOCUS STONE: Amazonite (green)

INTENTION STONES: Aquamarine (blue), citrine

PERIMETER STONES: Clear quartz points (magnifies)

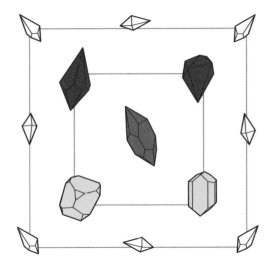

DECISIVENESS

When it comes to making decisions, your intuition and your heart are your best guides. These are the realms of the third eye chakra and heart chakra. Focusing especially on the third eye chakra connects you to higher guidance, which can help you make decisions that serve the highest and greatest good.

MANTRA

I give thanks to my intuition for guiding me to decisions that serve my highest and greatest good.

PRESCRIPTION #1—AMETHYST

Amethyst is one of the most powerful crystals for connecting you to your Divine guidance system. These hexagonal crystals amplify the messages that come from your higher self, making it easier for you to recognize them as wisdom and guidance.

When you need to make a decision, hold an amethyst in your receiving (nondominant) hand and visualize the choice you have to make.

Repeat the mantra and sit quietly until the answer to your question arises.

PRESCRIPTION #2—AMETRINE

Ametrine connects the third eye and solar plexus, drawing the energy through your heart as it moves between the two. This makes it an excellent crystal to use that allows you not only to make decisions based upon higher guidance, but also to make them based in love and compassion as well as gut instinct.

Lie on your back with a piece of ametrine halfway between your heart and throat chakra (on your upper chest).

Ask the question about the decision you have to make.

Visualize the energy moving upward from the solar plexus, passing through the heart, and into your third eye chakra.

Allow the information that comes through to guide you to a decision.

PRESCRIPTION #3—THIRD EYE GRID

Make a third eye grid with amethyst and clear quartz. Lay it out on your bedside table, ask your question before you go to sleep, and then sleep on it. The amethyst and clear quartz will help the answer come to you as you sleep. You can use any size and shape of stone.

CONFIGURATION: Eye

FOCUS STONE: Amethyst (a stone deeply connected to your third eye and intuition)

PERIMETER/INTENTION STONES: Clear quartz (magnifies)

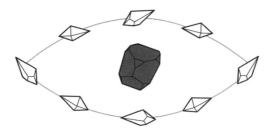

ENVY

Envy and its close cousin jealousy are emotions that keep you from moving forward on your path in peace and joy. Often, these emotions arise from the mistaken belief that if someone else has something, it means we can't or won't have it as well. Instead of focusing on what someone else has that you don't have, you can instead focus on what you choose to create.

MANTRA

I am creating the life I desire.

PRESCRIPTION #1—GREEN AVENTURINE

Envy is another energy of excess, so a stone that absorbs is the ideal choice. As clichéd as it may sound, green stones are ideal for releasing envy or jealousy. Green aventurine serves a dual purpose. It allows you to release envy and also supports personal goals.

Hold a green aventurine in your receiving (nondominant) hand and another in your giving (dominant) hand when you feel envious.

Visualize the envy as green smoke pouring from your body and into the stone in your receiving hand.

Once the envy has left your energy field, shift your focus to the stone in your receiving hand and repeat the mantra.

When you are done, place the stone from your receiving hand on the ground and let the energy absorb into the Earth, which will neutralize it.